Walks in

DACORUM

INTRODUCTION

This book is intended for anyone, especially families and retired people, interested in exploring the Dacorum area on foot. Each walk has a map and full directions, with notes about points of interest in a separate section at the back. The walks vary in length from three to eleven miles and cover all areas of the Borough.

'Walks in Dacorum' originated in 1985 as a series of leaflets devised for Dacorum Borough Council by staff on the Manpower Services Commission Community Programme Scheme. The first edition of the book was published in 1986. This new edition sets out to bring the walk descriptions up to date, to offer alternative routes for those walks affected by new road building, and to expand the information section.

The fieldwork for the walks revision was done in early 1992, but the features of the countryside can change rapidly and no responsibility can be accepted for changes since then. Where walks are affected by the new A41 bypasses (Kings Langley, Berkhamsted and Aston Clinton) the route described in the text is, as far as possible, as it will be after construction works are complete. Temporary diversions are described in a central pull-out section and the sections affected are indicated with an asterisk (*).

Many of the walks can be muddy in wet weather, especially where they follow bridleways - for example on the Ashridge Estate. Stout boots or shoes are recommended. Waterproof clothing is also advisable, given the vagaries of the English climate. Several of the walks cross golf courses : though all the walks follow recognised paths, please take care and show consideration to golfers. Walks can also be affected by ploughing or other temporary diversions, so please observe the Country Code and refer to Ordnance Survey maps if in doubt as to routes. Finally, please show consideration to local residents when parking cars: parking space is often limited, and private areas such as pub car parks should never be used without first seeking permission from the owner.

Happy Walking!

ACKNOWLEDGEMENTS

Thanks are due to all those involved in the original 'Walks in Dacorum' project : especially Alan Beaver, who took the photographs, Gina Spreckley, who drew the sketches, and Olive Bolton, who co-ordinated the project.

David Goode did much preliminary work checking the routes for this edition. I would like to thank him and also all those local groups and individuals who offered comments and suggestions, especially John Rowe, Tom Horne, Jonathan Lee and all those friends who shared the walks.

Isabel Jordan
Editor

FOLLOW THE COUNTRY CODE

Enjoy the countryside and respect its life and work.
Guard against all risk of fire.
Fasten all gates.
Keep your dog under close control.
Keep to public paths across farmland.
Use gates and stiles to cross fences, hedges and walls.
Leave livestock, crops and machinery alone.
Take your litter home.
Help to keep all water clean.
Protect wildlife, plants and trees.
Take special care on country roads.
Make no unnecessary noise.

MAPS

The following maps cover the Dacorum area in more detail, and are recommended as companions to the route descriptions and sketch maps.

Ordnance Survey 'Landranger' series (1:50 000) :
165 : Aylesbury & Leighton Buzzard area
166 : Luton, Hertford and surrounding area

Ordnance Survey 'Pathfinder' series (1:25 000) :
1094 : Aylesbury & Tring
1095 : Harpenden
1118 : Chesham & Wendover
1119 : St Albans & Hemel Hempstead

HOW TO USE THIS BOOK

Each walk has a route description and sketch map which are designed to be used together. The paragraph numbers in the text refer to the numbers appearing on the map : for ease of use the starting point on the map is highlighted. The boldface numbers in the right hand margin of the text refer to sections in the 'Places of Interest' listing at the back of the book.

FOREWORD

One of the many good things about living in Dacorum is how easy it is to get into the countryside, so much of it unspoilt. The best way to explore it is on foot, keeping to public rights of way, and observing the Country Code. This book is to help you with that exploration. It suggests 33 round walks, each with places to park, and often with a pub somewhere on the route.

The walks cover all sorts of terrain, and between them will take you to the most interesting rural sights in our Borough. They offer you gentle - or more vigorous - exercise; ever-changing views of our Chiltern landscape; new perspectives on familiar scenes; contact with nature at close quarters.

As we move through the countryside we can see how it came by its present shape and many various textures : the titanic struggle that raised and folded the chalk sea bed; the weather, that smoothed the hills and gouged the valleys; the countless interactions of plant and worm, insect and bird; the earliest human activity of which faint traces survive; then thousands of years of felling, clearing, draining, ploughing, planting, pasturing, ditching, hedging and coppicing; the crescendo of building and engineering works in the last two centuries; sadly, here and there, abuse, exploitation and neglect. Our countryside needs us to cherish and protect it, and we will do that more effectively the better we know and understand it.

Since the first edition of this book, I have walked most of the routes it describes, some of them several times. I can thoroughly recommend this updated edition as a reliable guide, easy to follow, and packed with useful, interesting information.

Keith Hunt

CHIEF EXECUTIVE   April 1992

CONTENTS

	Page
Key to maps & abbreviations	front cover
Introduction / Acknowledgements	2
Country Code / Maps / How to use this book	3
Foreword	4
Walk 1 : Little Gaddesden - Ashridge	6/7
Walk 2 : Wilstone - Tring Reservoirs	8/9
Walk 3 : Tring - Hastoe - Tring Park	10/11
Walk 4 : Berkhamsted - Berkhamsted Common	12/13
Walk 5 : Dudswell - Northchurch Common	14/15
Walk 6 : Ashridge - Aldbury - Pitstone Hill	16/17
Walk 7 : Wigginton - Cholesbury	18/19
Walk 8 : Bridgewater Monument - South Ashridge	20/21
Walk 9 : Wilstone - Puttenham - Buckland	24/25
Walk 10 : Wilstone - Marsworth - Long Marston	26/27
Walk 11 : Bridgewater Monument - Ivinghoe Beacon	28/29
Walk 12 : Berkhamsted - Bourne End - Ashley Green	30/31
Walk 13 : Jockey End - Flamstead	32/33
Walk 14 : Great Gaddesden - Jockey End	34/35
Walk 15 : Gaddesden Row - Bridens Camp	36/37
Walk 16 : Potten End - Great Gaddesden - Nettleden	38/39
Walk 17 : Markyate - Pepperstock - Flamstead	42/43
Walk 18 : Potten End - Frithsden Copse	44/45
Walk 19 : Hemel Hempstead Old Town - Piccotts End	46/47
Walks in Dacorum : General Map	48/49
Temporary Diversions	supplementary pages
Walk 20 : Boxmoor - Winkwell - Hemel Hempstead	50/51
Walk 21 : Jockey End - Studham	52/53
Walk 22 : Great Gaddesden - Hudnall Common - Studham	54/55
Walk 23 : Markyate - Studham	56/57
Walk 24 : Chipperfield - Belsize	58/59
Walk 25 : Chipperfield - Flaunden	60/61
Walk 26 : Felden - Bovingdon	62/63
Walk 27 : Flaunden - Chess Valley	66/67
Walk 28 : Kings Langley - Apsley	68/69
Walk 29 : Bovingdon Green - Flaunden - Ley Hill Common	70/71
Walk 30 : Chipperfield Common - Langley Lodge	72/73
Walk 31 : Nash Mills - Bedmond	74/75
Walk 32 : Boxmoor - Little Hay - Winkwell	76/77
Walk 33 : Apsley - Scatterdells Wood	78/79
Places of Interest	80
Further Information	back cover

WALK 1

**LENGTH: 3½ MILES
or 3 MILES
TIME: 2 HOURS
or 1½ HOURS**

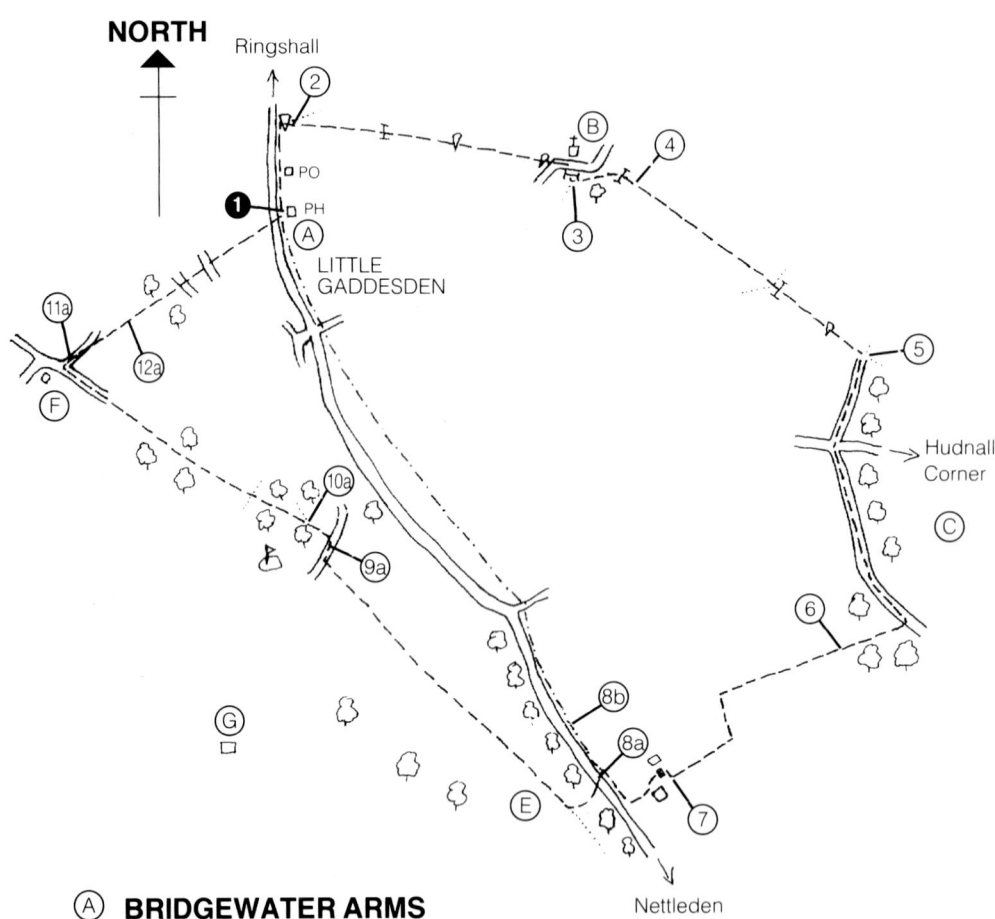

- Ⓐ **BRIDGEWATER ARMS**
- Ⓑ **LITTLE GADDESDEN CHURCH**
- Ⓒ **HUDNALL COMMON**
- Ⓓ **LITTLE GADDESDEN COMMON**
- Ⓔ **GOLDEN VALLEY**
- Ⓕ **ELECTRICITY SUB-STATION**
- Ⓖ **ASHRIDGE COLLEGE**

LITTLE GADDESDEN - ASHRIDGE   *WALK 1*

Park in LITTLE GADDESDEN, near the Bridgewater Arms PH (A) (GR SP992 136). Occasional buses stop here.   **31**

1. Facing PH, turn left towards Ringshall, pass the village Post Office/Stores and turn right at kissing gate (SP to Church of St Peter & St Paul).
2. Bear right and cross field to stile. Continue on well-defined path, through two kissing gates, to road in front of CHURCH (B). A brief visit to the church is recommended.   **31.1**
3. Opposite entrance to church is a stile with two SPs. Follow SP to Hudnall Common. Keep tree on RHS and cross field to next stile, which is difficult to spot until nearing fence.
4. Over stile on to footpath running along headland of next field with hedge on LHS. Over another stile and keep to LH edge of field. At far corner go through kissing gate and down narrow alleyway to a private road.
5. Turn right and after about 200 yards cross over main road onto another private road. Presently open space on the left gives views across HUDNALL COMMON (C) and beyond. On the right opposite take bridleway (SP) into trees.
6. On emerging from copse the path goes between wire fence on LHS and hedge on RHS, and then bends left to follow edge of field. Turn right on wide path towards farm buildings.
7. Entering farm area turn right at brick wall and almost immediately left through a metal gate under a willow tree. Go down narrow path and onto concrete drive to main road. Turn right on pavement.

8a. LONGER ROUTE : Walk along pavement for about 150 yards, then at SP on LHS cross road. Take path down hill through trees into GOLDEN VALLEY (E). Turn right along grassy valley bottom to reach a road.
9a. At road turn right. Walk along verge for about 150 yards and turn left onto an unmarked wide track through trees.
10a. Follow track up hill and fork left along footpath. Keep golf course fairway on RHS and continue as path curves slightly to left through trees and becomes grassy and flint based. Path leads to gravelled road which soon turns to tarmac.
11a. Just before junction with road on left, and with electricity sub-station ("Captain Downer") on LHS (F), turn right on surfaced drive for a few yards before bearing right on grass path between house gardens.
12a. Continue through trees, across a golf tee, and descend through a wood. Path goes straight on between posts and along a narrow alley to another set of posts. Cross two private roads and follow another alley beside a paddock and field. A last walk-through stile leads to Bridgewater Arms car park.

8b. SHORTER ROUTE : Follow pavement to T-junction. Take footpath across Little Gaddesden COMMON (D) to War Memorial and then on beside road for 200 yards to Bridgewater Arms. It is sometimes possible to see ASHRIDGE COLLEGE (G) from the Memorial.   **31.2**
  4.3

WALK 2

LENGTH: 4 MILES
TIME: 2 HOURS

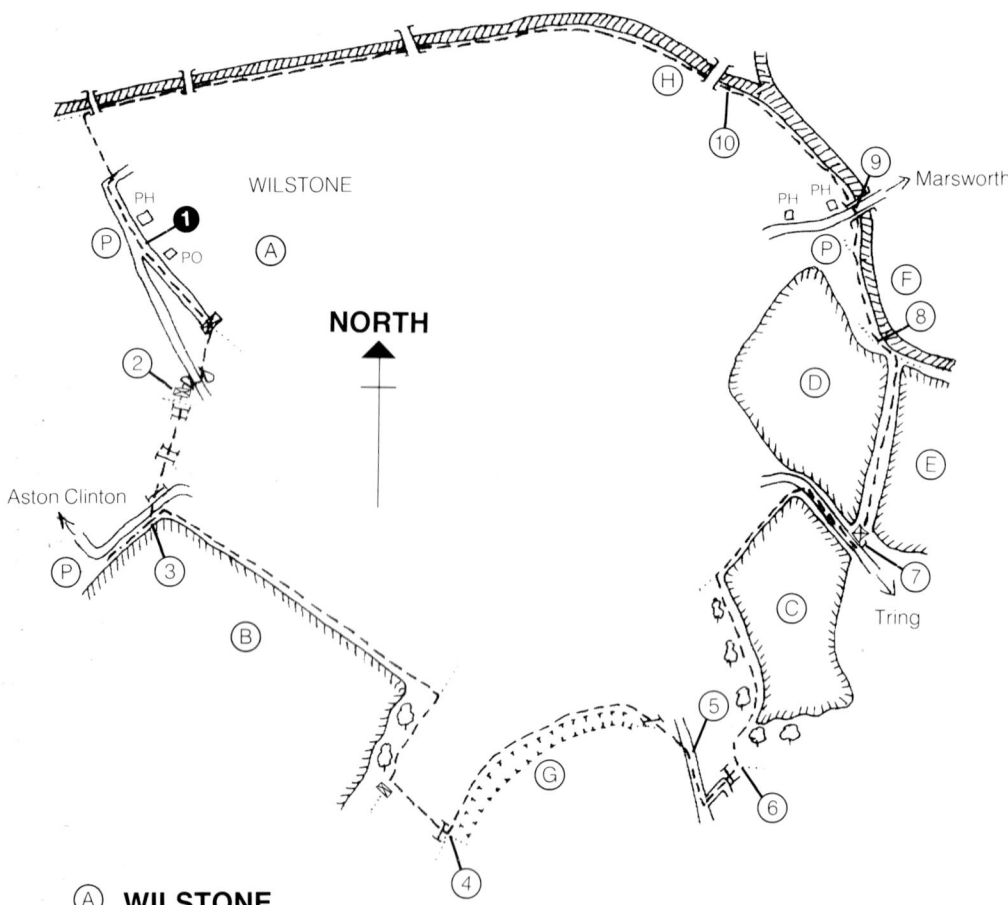

- Ⓐ **WILSTONE**
- Ⓑ **WILSTONE RESERVOIR**
- Ⓒ **TRINGFORD RESERVOIR**
- Ⓓ **STARTOPS END RESERVOIR**
- Ⓔ **MARSWORTH RESERVOIR**
- Ⓕ **GRAND UNION CANAL**
- Ⓖ **WENDOVER ARM**
- Ⓗ **AYLESBURY ARM**

WILSTONE - TRING RESERVOIRS *WALK 2*

Park (P) in WILSTONE VILLAGE (A), near The Half Moon PH (GR SP904 141). The village has a limited bus service. Alternative parking is available beside WILSTONE RESERVOIR (GR SP903 134) : if parking here join the walk at Section 3.
It is also possible to park at STARTOPS END RESERVOIR (GR SP919 141) and join the walk at Section 9.   **45**

1. Facing PH turn right, then fork left with bus shelter on RHS. Pass village Post Office/Stores on LHS and follow cul-de-sac to end. Through gate, cross field diagonally right to kissing gate. Cross road, then slightly to right go through two kissing gates with footbridge between and cross corner of paddock.

2. Go through wooden gate, cross farm track and then over two stiles and FB. Cross field diagonally right, negotiating double wooden fence in middle of field. At far corner of field cross stile onto road, and cross road to high embankment ahead.

3. Climb embankment either at corner or up path from car park area to right. Turn left, with WILSTONE RESERVOIR (B) on RHS, and follow path to T-junction with track. Turn right along track, with trees on RHS beside reservoir. At gate turn left on path which runs uphill between two hedges to stile and path junction.   **23.2**

4. Turn left (ignore paths ahead and to right) and follow path beside dry canal. This is the WENDOVER ARM (G) of the Grand Union Canal. After about ¼ mile a stile leads to a track down to the road.   **23.1**

5. Turn right on road for about 150 yards. Turn left onto a private road and after 100 yards cross stile ahead. The pumping station which controls the water level in the Grand Union Canal is high up on RHS.

6. Take left path into wood adjoining TRINGFORD RESERVOIR (C). Keep reservoir on RHS and follow path, which can be muddy in wet conditions, round to road. Turn right on pavement with hedge on RHS for 100 yards.

7. At the end of pavement cross road and turn back to the left, over a stile/gate into Coarse Fishing Area. Follow path between two reservoirs, STARTOPS END (D) on LHS and MARSWORTH (E) on RHS.

8. The GRAND UNION CANAL (F) appears ahead. Turn left, and after a few yards take path on right to descend a slight bank and join towpath. Do not take path into car park but continue on towpath to road bridge and lock with two PHs on LHS : The White Lion and The Angler's Retreat.

9. Cross road and descend again to towpath, with canal still on RHS. At canal junction remain on towpath to follow lefthand canal, the AYLESBURY ARM (H).

10. Continue on towpath for about a mile, passing under three bridges and beside seven locks. At footbridge over canal turn left, along side of playing field to road. Turn right on road and follow round to left into Wilstone village.

WALK 3

**LENGTH: 4½ MILES
or 3½ MILES
TIME: 2½ HOURS
or 2 HOURS**

- Ⓐ **CHURCH**
- Ⓑ **MUSEUM**
- Ⓒ **STUBBINGS WOOD**
- Ⓓ **OBELISK**
- Ⓔ **MANSION**

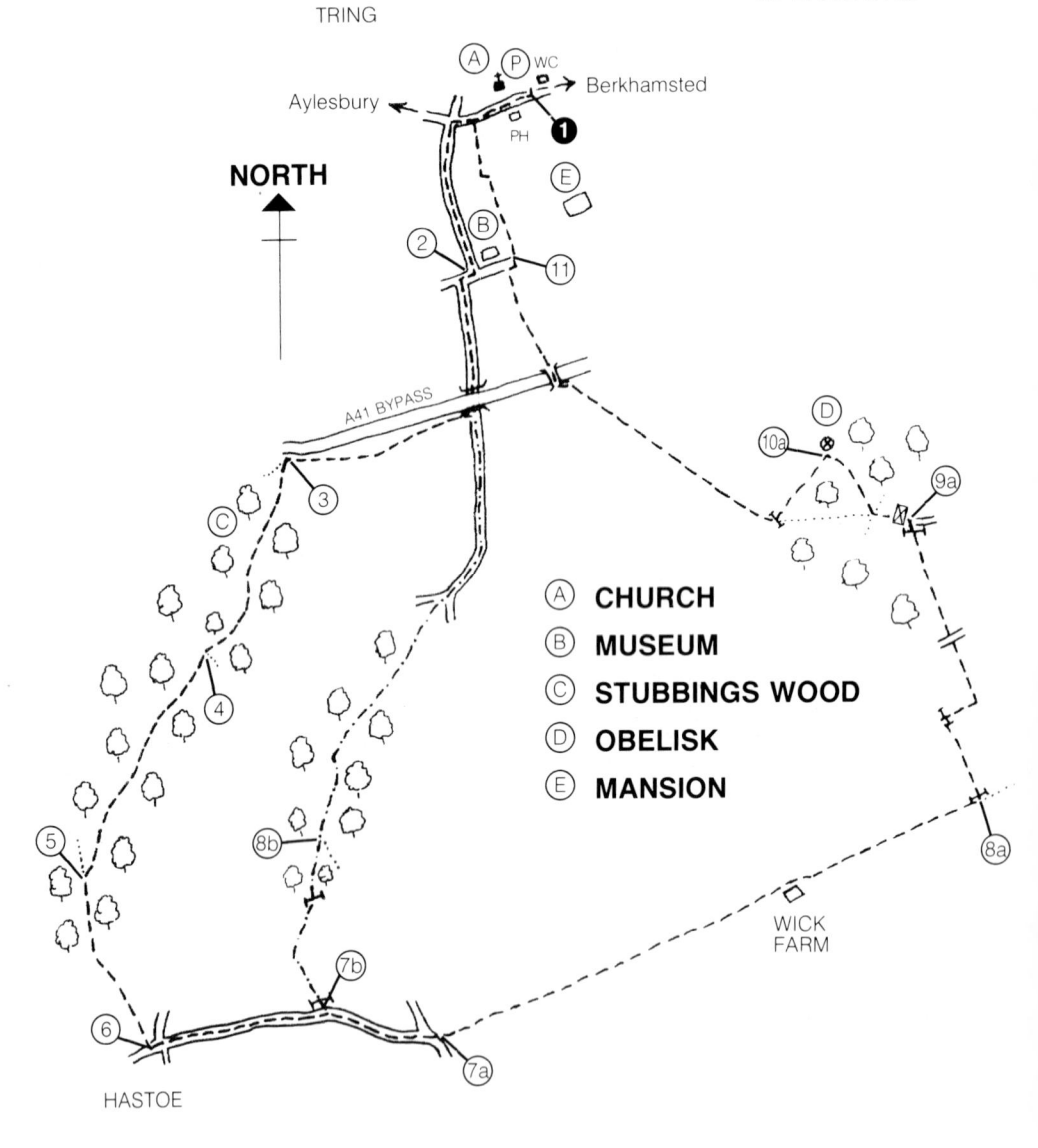

TRING - HASTOE - TRING PARK   WALK 3

Park in TRING MAIN CAR PARK (P) (GR SP 925 115) - not Thursday afternoons or Fridays. Buses stop nearby.   **43**

1. From car park turn right along High Street for 200 yards, passing CHURCH (A) on RHS. At crossroads turn left into Akeman St and continue past ZOOLOGICAL MUSEUM (B).   **43.1**
43.6

2. At junction turn right and then left up Hastoe Lane, under bypass. At SP to Hastoe turn right through gate and follow footpath beside bypass to STUBBINGS WOOD (C). Note view of Tring and beyond from highest point of path.   **43.4**

3. In wood bear left on path, then immediately turn left at path junction. Follow narrow path uphill (steep at first) to clearing and then path junction.

4. Take RH fork and keeping on roughly the same contour continue on wide track for about ¼ mile. Note extensive gale damage to trees, with views over Aylesbury Vale through gaps.

5. When track drops down to sunken bridleway, turn left on bridleway and follow out of woods and along wider track to Hastoe.

6. At road junction turn left to follow Church Lane (SP RIDGEWAY PATH) for about ¼ mile to stile and SP on left.   **40**

7a. LONGER ROUTE : Continue along Church Lane to road junction. Follow Ridgeway Path SPs straight on along track, passing Wick Farm on RHS.

8a. Just before reaching houses (Wigginton village) turn left over stile (Ridgeway Path SP). Take path between fences and turn right over another stile leading to path behind houses. Path bends left, then through wooden barriers over a private road and on to another stile.

9a. Over this stile turn left through a gate (away from Ridgeway Path). Follow path about 100 yards into woods, to next path junction. Take path ahead which bears slightly to right and leads downhill for 200 yards to OBELISK (D).   **43.3**

10a. Leaving Obelisk on RHS turn left down avenue to gate into Tring Park. Over gate/stile turn right, following path between fences to footbridge over bypass. Note views of MANSION (E) across bypass. Cross bridge, then along path to road and cross to alley opposite (SP).   **43.2**

7b. SHORTER ROUTE : Over stile and follow SP direction with remnant of hedge on RHS. At wooden fence bear right, keeping fence on LHS, and continue to stile on left into wood. Over stile, path bends to right and descends to junction with track.

8b. Turn left and follow track down hill and through recently cleared area to stile leading onto road. Across the road take tarmac footpath, then continue down lane, under bypass bridge, to road junction. Turn right, then after about 100 yards left into alley (SP).

11. Walk down alley behind Museum, through left/right dogleg to High Street and turn right to return to car park.

WALK 4

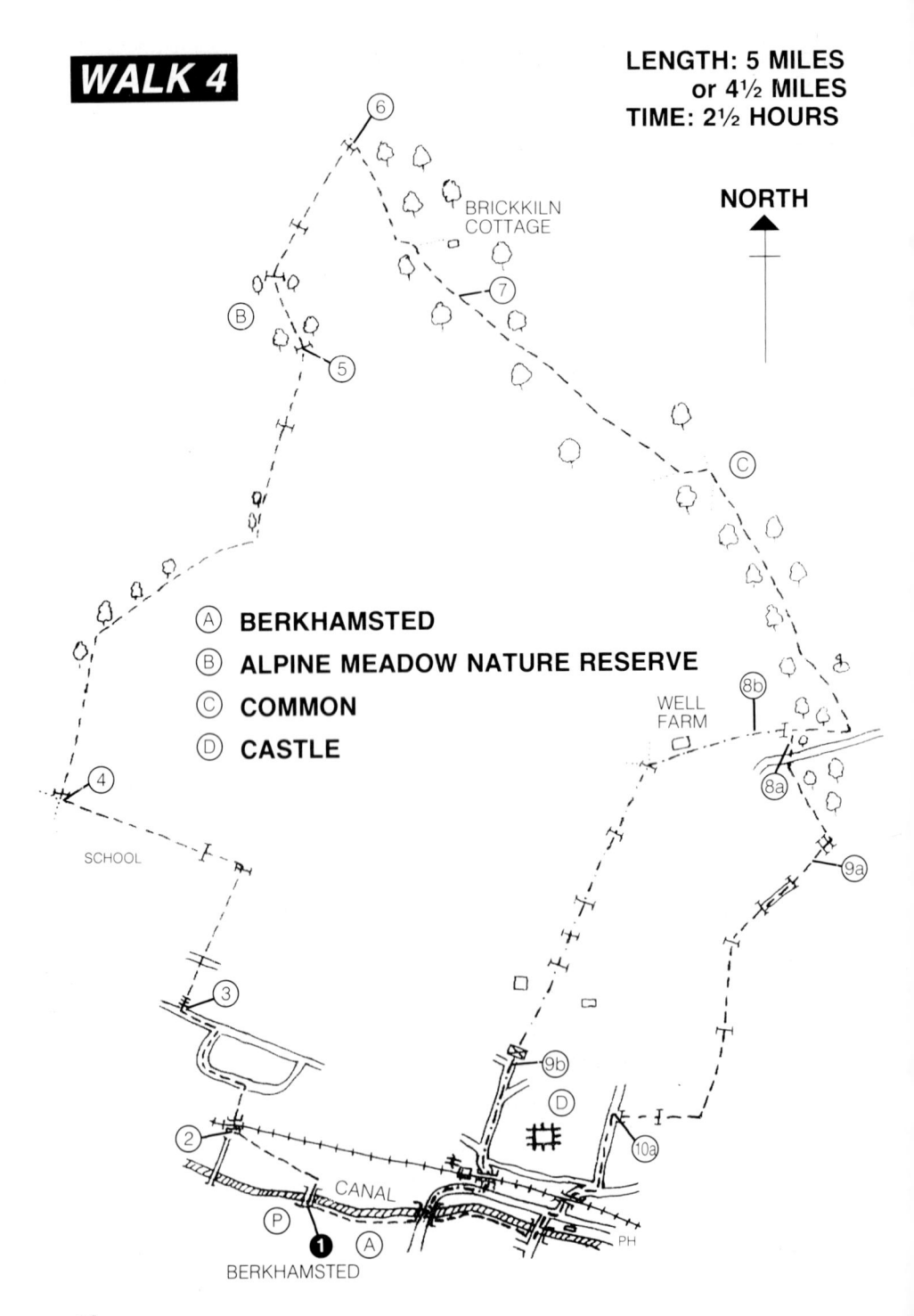

LENGTH: 5 MILES or 4½ MILES
TIME: 2½ HOURS

NORTH

BRICKKILN COTTAGE

Ⓐ **BERKHAMSTED**
Ⓑ **ALPINE MEADOW NATURE RESERVE**
Ⓒ **COMMON**
Ⓓ **CASTLE**

WELL FARM

SCHOOL

CANAL

BERKHAMSTED

12

BERKHAMSTED - BERKHAMSTED COMMON **WALK 4**

Park in car park (P) at St John's Well Lane, BERKHAMSTED (A) (GR SP989 081), about ½ mile west from Berkhamsted BR station. 7

1. From car park take wooden bridge over RIVER BULBOURNE and GRAND UNION CANAL, then turn left. Pass between play area and Bowls Club and cross open field to end of the next canal footbridge. 13 23.1

2. Walk under railway bridge and on between houses. Turn left at road (South Park Gardens) and follow RH curve to T junction. Turn left on Bridgewater Rd and after approx 100 yards cross over to take FP (SP) up steps with handrail.

3. Follow path up hill, cross one road and then on between house gardens, finally passing school playing field on LHS. At stile at top of path turn left, then over another stile and straight on along path with hedge on RHS and school on LHS. Continue to next stile on right.

4. Turn right over stile and keep to edge of field with hedge on LHS for about ½ mile. At end of field follow path as it bears round to left through gap in hedge, keeping belt of trees, then hedge on LHS. Over next stile and follow line of trees downhill to stile on left at entrance to woods.

5. Follow path for short distance through woods, then uphill into clearing (ALPINE MEADOW NATURE RESERVE (B)) and into further belt of trees. Over stile and on with hedge on LHS to next stile. Continue through second field to stile in LH corner. 7.3

6. Over stile turn right on path parallel with edge of field, passing close to stable buildings. At gate on RHS at corner of field, bear left along gravel track. After about 100 yards turn right on narow path near edge of copse. Path may be indistinct but keeps about 100 yards downhill from house and roughly follows contour, with woods on RHS.

7. Continue through bracken for about ½ mile, noting variety of trees and looking out for deer. When path veers left and meets bridleway, bear right (not downhill) and follow track for another ½ mile. Pass between golf green and tee, but just before road take path downhill to right through trees.

8a. LONGER ROUTE : At path junction in woods turn left to road. Cross road to find unmarked path opposite, which runs uphill through woods close to field fence. At top of path turn right (before houses) and over pair of stiles.

9a. Keep to top edge of field, along stretch of concrete path with cattle grids/stiles at each end and then on through two further gates/stiles. Note views of TOWN (A) ahead and COMMON (C) behind and to right. At corner of last field turn right and follow hedge on LHS, over two stiles and down to road. 7.4 7.2

10a. Cross road and turn left, noting CASTLE (D). Follow road under narrow railway bridge, turn right and then left over canal bridge. Take footpath down to join canal towpath and continue past one bridge and lock to car park access. 7.1

8b. SHORTER ROUTE : Follow path down through trees to stile. Over stile continue straight on down farm track, passing Well Farm on RHS. At bottom of hill (often very wet and muddy) take footpath to left over stile. Continue with hedge on RHS over next four stiles, then between sports fields and through car park.

9b. At road go straight on towards BR station, passing CASTLE (D) on LHS. Under railway bridge, turn right and follow road as it curves left. Over canal bridge and take steps down to towpath. Turn left past lock and continue to car park access. 7.1

13

WALK 5

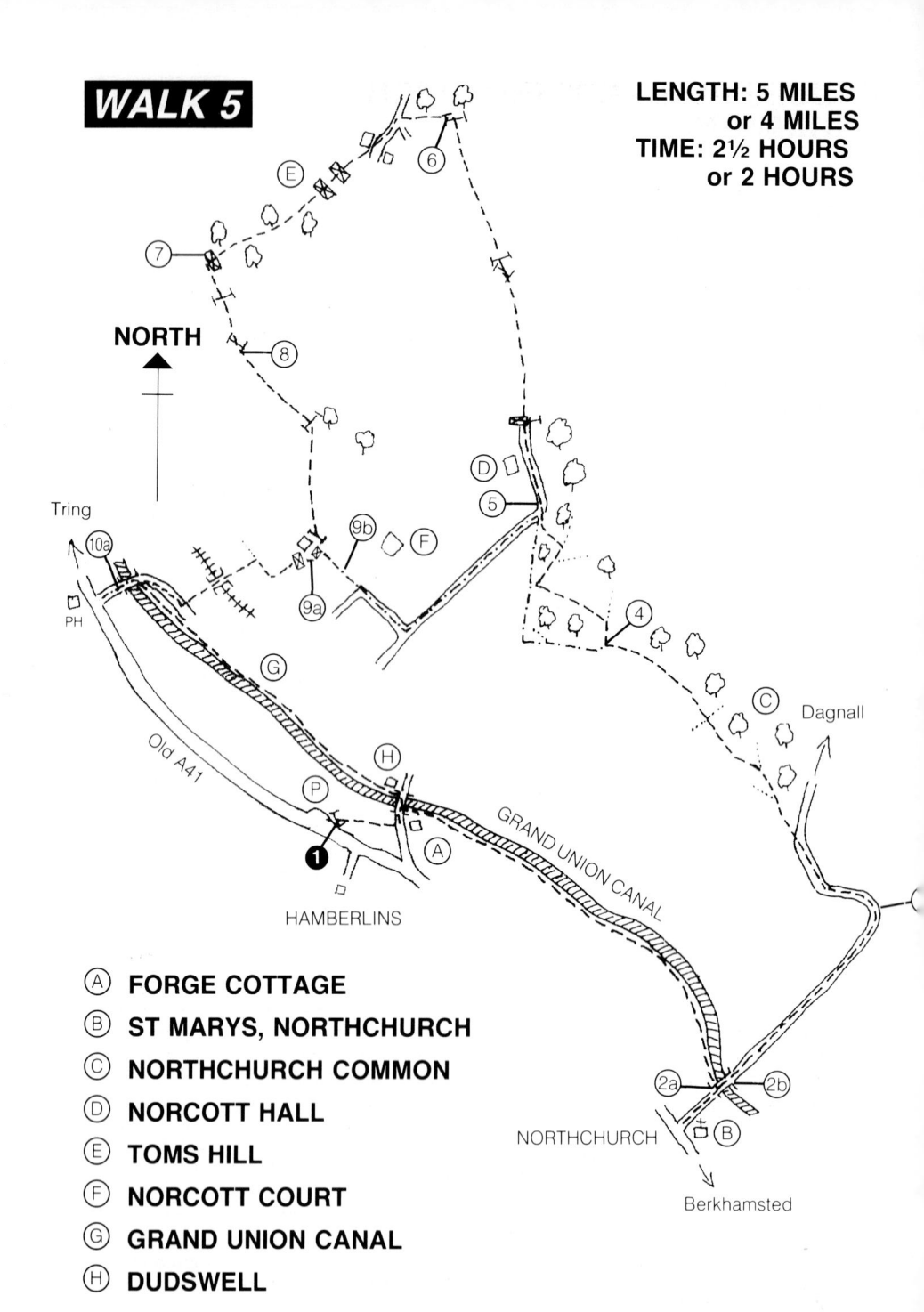

LENGTH: 5 MILES
or 4 MILES
TIME: 2½ HOURS
or 2 HOURS

NORTH

Tring

Old A41

HAMBERLINS

GRAND UNION CANAL

NORTHCHURCH

Berkhamsted

Dagnall

- Ⓐ **FORGE COTTAGE**
- Ⓑ **ST MARYS, NORTHCHURCH**
- Ⓒ **NORTHCHURCH COMMON**
- Ⓓ **NORCOTT HALL**
- Ⓔ **TOMS HILL**
- Ⓕ **NORCOTT COURT**
- Ⓖ **GRAND UNION CANAL**
- Ⓗ **DUDSWELL**

DUDSWELL - NORTHCHURCH COMMON *WALK 5*

Park in lay-by (P) beside old A41, 200 yards west of entrance to Hamberlin's Hotel at Dudswell (GR SP963 096). Nearest bus stop (limited weekday service only) at Cow Roast,½ mile west. For shorter alternative route park on Northchurch Common (GR SP979 094), and start walk at Section 3.

1. From the lay-by, cross the stile at footpath SP. Cross the field diagonally right to a path entrance between two houses; follow to road. This is DUDSWELL village and opposite is FORGE COTTAGE (A). Turn left on road and then right on towpath. Follow towpath with CANAL on LHS to the next bridge, at Northchurch.

19.1
23.1

2a. To visit ST MARY'S, NORTHCHURCH (B), turn right on road to T- junction. Retrace steps to end of Section 1.

36.1

2b. From canal bridge walk uphill on pavement beside road to Dagnall as far as first bend in road.

3. For shorter alternative route, start here. Continue beside road for about 400 yards, and just before deer warning sign cross road to take path (SP) on left through trees (C). 200 yards ahead fork right, at next path junction turn left, and follow path downhill to track. Cross over track onto an uphill path, which later descends to a small clearing.

4. Take right fork (ignoring waymarks ahead), and after about 200 yards turn left up a wide grass incline. At top turn right. Ignore wide path to right, but about 50 yards beyond turn left on path through trees onto track which leads to road.

5. Go straight on along private road, past NORCOTT HALL and farm (D) on LHS to white gates and stile. Over stile, continue with hedge, then fence on RHS to further stile. Cross, and immediately turn left through gate and stile. With hedge on LHS continue to end of field and over stile.

6. Turn left and follow path to road. Ignore private drive and turn left on road, passing between buildings. After house on RHS bear right onto track and follow this through two gates. Track enters wood (E) and descends to gate.

7. Go through gate into field and turn left. Cross stile into next field and follow path diagonally right, down to trees. Cross stile about half way along bottom edge of field. Bear left to gap in hedge, then turn left along edge of field with hedge on LHS.

8. Continue across open field on path towards trees. Cross stile into next field, then cross field diagonally right towards farm buildings. Note NORCOTT COURT (F) to LHS. Cross stile in corner of field near farm, then turn left through gate/stile on to farm road.

9a. LONGER ROUTE : Turn right almost immediately after farm gate and take track through another gate. After about 200 yards the track veers right. 100 yards further on turn left onto path across an open field. Cross railway footbridge and then further field to road. Turn right to bridge over GRAND UNION CANAL (G).

10a. To visit COW ROAST INN, cross bridge and take road ahead to main road. Retrace steps. Drop down to canal towpath, turn under bridge and with canal on RHS continue past one lock to bridge and lock at DUDSWELL (H). Cross bridge and after 100 yards turn right at SP between houses to return to lay-by.

19

9b. SHORTER ROUTE : Go straight on along farm track and then at junction continue on road. At next junction turn left (SP Berkhamsted Common). At top of hill, when road turns left, take path on right through trees. At path junction fork right and follow path until it bears left to join wider path. Turn right down hill to reach clearing at end of Section 3. Retrace steps to road.

15

WALK 6

LENGTH: 5½ MILES
TIME: 3 HOURS

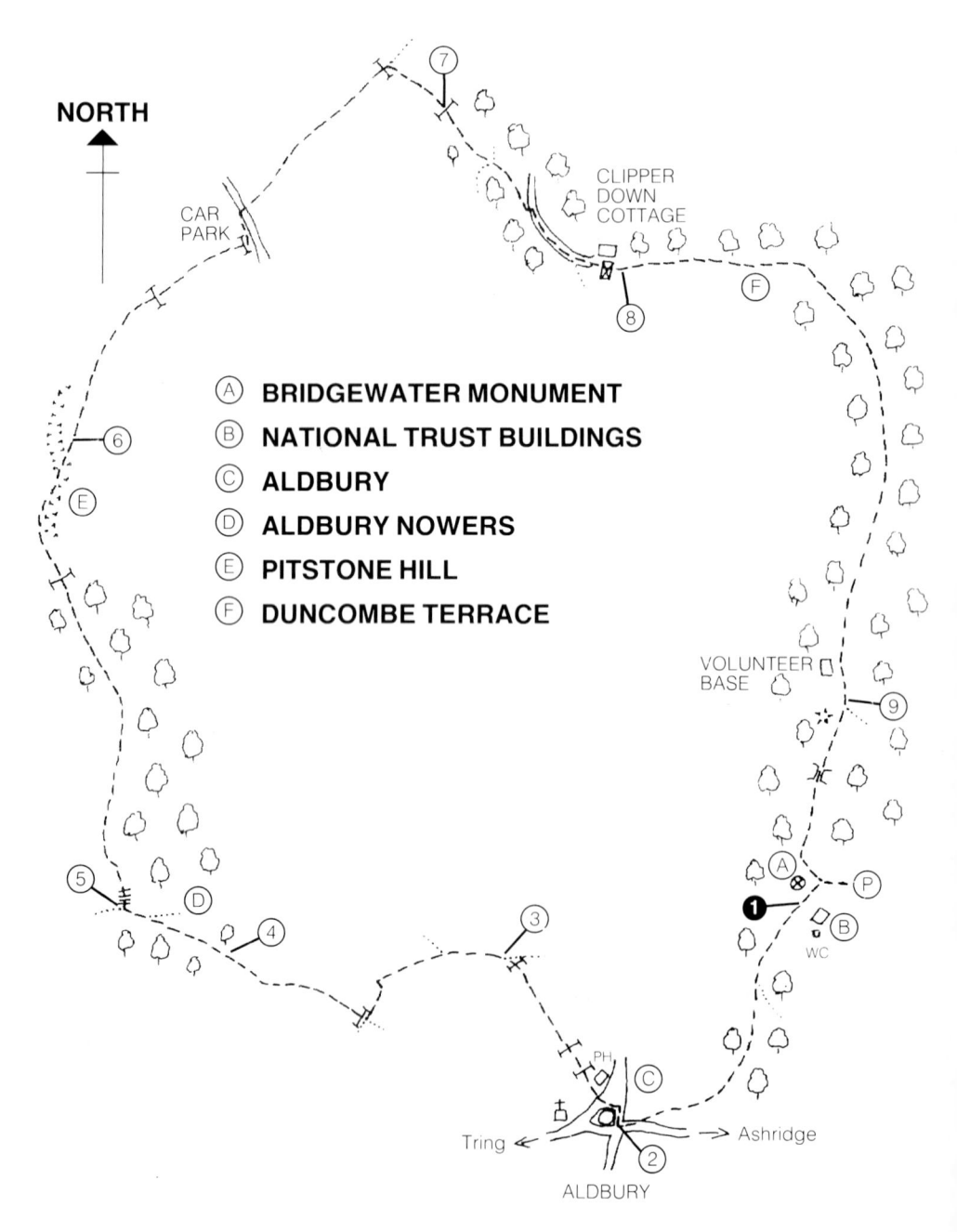

NORTH

- Ⓐ BRIDGEWATER MONUMENT
- Ⓑ NATIONAL TRUST BUILDINGS
- Ⓒ ALDBURY
- Ⓓ ALDBURY NOWERS
- Ⓔ PITSTONE HILL
- Ⓕ DUNCOMBE TERRACE

CAR PARK

CLIPPER DOWN COTTAGE

VOLUNTEER BASE

WC

Tring ← ALDBURY → Ashridge

16

ASHRIDGE - ALDBURY - PITSTONE HILL   **WALK 6**

Park (P) at the BRIDGEWATER MONUMENT (A) off B4506, main Northchurch - Ringshall road (GR SP970 131). A charge is made for parking at weekends. No regular public transport is available.   **4.1**

1. With the MONUMENT on RHS follow path to left leaving NATIONAL TRUST BUILDINGS (B) on LHS. Descend wide track through the trees (ignore path to left on level contour). Continue for about ½ mile, past houses on LHS, to road. Turn right into ALDBURY village (C).   **4.2**

   1.1

2. Turn right and at far end of village pond follow SP arrow pointing to entrance opposite, with PH on RHS. Take path between wooden fence and brick wall, then turn right over stile. Cross school field diagonally to far corner, then over stile continue on same line across large field.

3. Cross stile and turn left along bridleway. Pass FP sign on RHS and follow bridleway which bends left and then right. At path junction cross stile on right and cross an open field towards woods. Go through a gap into next field and follow hedge on RHS.

4. At gap into corner of STRAWBERRY WOODS, the first part of ALDBURY NOWERS (D), take path into trees. Note areas of tree regeneration following storm damage. Continue to junction with track and turn left to meet the RIDGEWAY PATH (RP).   **1.4**

   40

5. Turn right up steps and follow RP acorn waymarks through woods, noting chalk grassland reserve on LHS with views to TRING and the VALE OF AYLESBURY. Cross next stile and follow RP as it curves gently round to the top of PITSTONE HILL (E), with Pitstone Cement Works to LHS.   **1.4**

6. From the top of the hill take path close to fence on RHS to next stile, then on to stile into car park. Turn left through car park then right out of entrance and cross road. Continue along RP across an open field. Over next stile turn right (leaving RP which goes straight on) and keep fence on RHS to next stile.

7. Over stile climb path through scrub area, with fence on RHS. When this path meets a track, continue up hill to junction with lane. Turn right along lane and when it bears left go through gate with cottage on LHS (ignore right fork which goes down hill).

8. Follow track past cottage. In wet conditions the next sections can be very muddy. The track continues for about a mile through the National Trust Ashridge Estate, around DUNCOMBE TERRACE (F) with views over Duncombe Farm and beyond.   **4.2**

9. Shortly after passing a building on RHS, the track veers left to a path junction. Take track to right, over a wooden footbridge and on to reach the open grass area and MONUMENT.

17

WALK 7

LENGTH: 6 MILES
TIME: 3 HOURS

- Ⓐ **GRIMS DITCH**
- Ⓑ **CHOLESBURY CAMP**
- Ⓒ **WINDMILL**

18

WIGGINTON - CHOLESBURY   **WALK 7**

Park in car park (P) next to play area/sports field in WIGGINTON village **44**
(GR SP938 099). Wigginton has a Monday - Saturday bus service only.

1. From the car park turn right and walk along the main road to Chesham. Pass sign to Wigginton Bottom on LHS and about 300 yards further on turn right over stile.
2. Cross field and over next stile turn right. After a few yards turn left across open field along a wide grassy track which joins belt of trees. Follow course of GRIMS DITCH (A) on LHS and continue through trees to stile onto road. **24**
3. Cross road and over stile take right hand path beside Grims Ditch (SP). Continue through wood to a gap ahead into an open field. Straight across field to hedge on far side.
4. Through gap in hedge, turn left and follow wide vehicle track. Continue as it enters woodland, where it can be very muddy. After about $\frac{1}{3}$ mile, when further woodland appears on RHS, cross a stile to right. Take path through woods to a stile onto road.
5. Turn right along road for about 150 yards, then turn left along bridleway, which is also often muddy. At corner of field on LHS, cross stile on left. Take path running parallel to field through edge of wood.
6. Follow path through wood (ignore stile on RHS leading to farm) and bear round to left. Cross stile on right into field where there are often horses. Cross to RH corner of field and another stile.
7. Take path through woods to next stile, where it emerges into scrub area. Continue through, ignoring track to right.
8. Path leads directly to earthworks of CHOLESBURY FORT (B). Go straight **16.1**
over ditch and over stile, then with pond on RHS to further gate/stile. (Do not turn right into churchyard). Follow track about 100 yards to road.
9. Turn left on main Cholesbury-Chesham road and walk along grass verge, crossing road to Tring and passing cricket pitch. Note WINDMILL (C) behind **16.2**
buildings across road.
10. Opposite The Full Moon PH, turn left down hill on path which skirts round house on RHS, enters trees and then meets wide track along bottom of hill.
11. Locate gap in hedge near path junction, and follow path uphill along LH edge of field. Cross one stile, and keeping to field edge descend to surfaced track in valley.
12. Turn left and follow track along the valley to road. Cross to stile into wood and take RH path (SP Wigginton). Shortly after entering conifer plantation turn left and follow this smaller path to path junction at edge of wood.
13. Turn right out of plantation and immediately left to cross stile into open field. Follow path diagonally right to next stile, then cross next field on same line. Turn right over stile and retrace steps to Wigginton.

WALK 8

LENGTH: 5 MILES
TIME: 2 HOURS

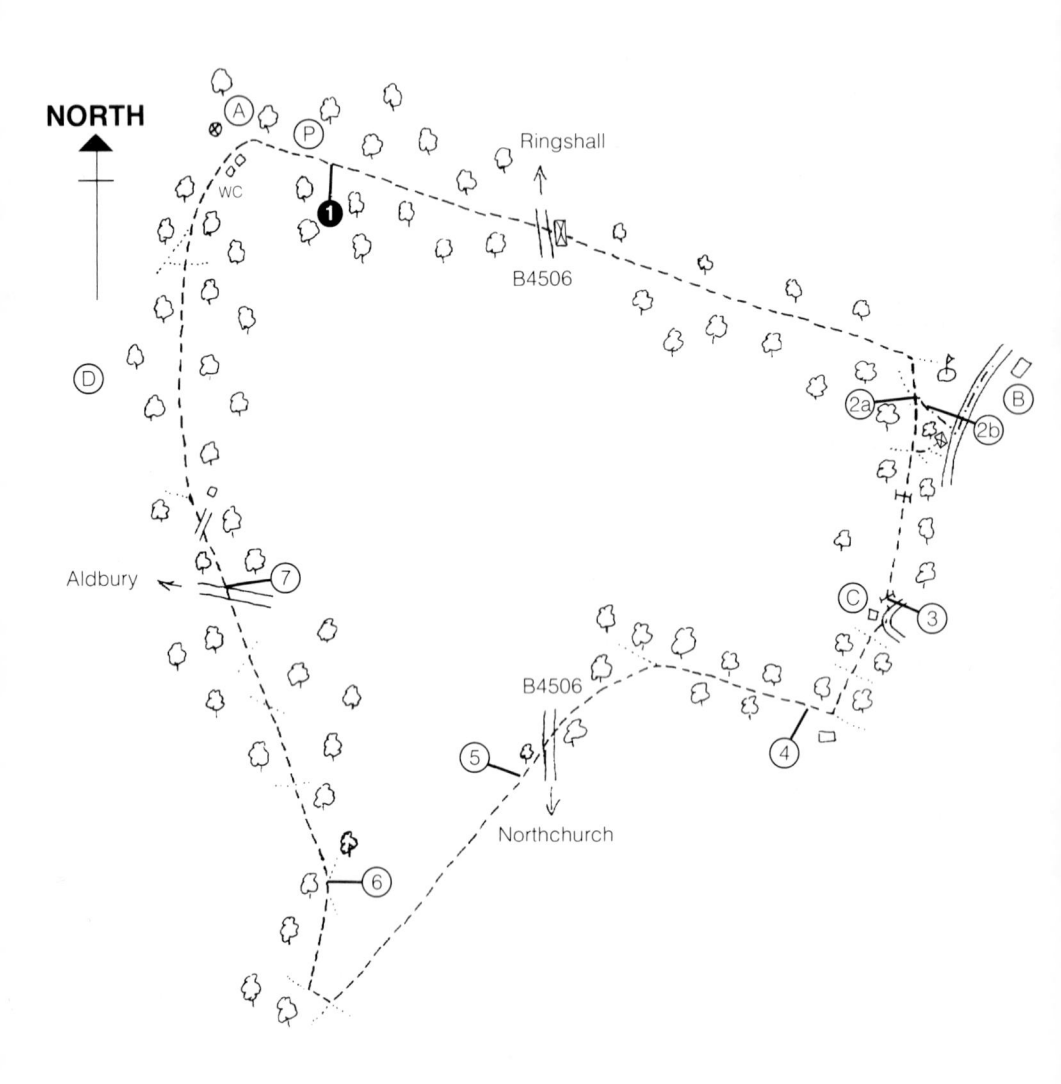

NORTH

Ringshall
B4506
Aldbury
B4506
Northchurch

- Ⓐ **BRIDGEWATER MONUMENT**
- Ⓑ **ASHRIDGE COLLEGE**
- Ⓒ **WOODYARD COTTAGES**
- Ⓓ **ALDBURY**

BRIDGEWATER MONUMENT - SOUTH ASHRIDGE

WALK 8

Park (P) at the BRIDGEWATER MONUMENT (A) off B4506, main Northchurch - Ringshall road (GR SP970 131). A charge is made for parking at weekends. No regular public transport is available. **4.1**

1. From MONUMENT (A), turn back down avenue and cross road. Go through gate and along grassy avenue towards ASHRIDGE COLLEGE (B). On reaching fence, turn right along path with golf course on LHS. **4.3**

2a. Follow waymarks across bridleway and over further track. Continue through trees to stile into open parkland. Over stile, bear slightly left to stile in bottom LH corner.

2b. Alternatively, to visit Ashridge College, turn left along bridleway to road. Turn left to College. Return to gated track to left of bridleway, and follow this for about 150 yards, until it is crossed by an indistinct footpath just past second track junction on left. Turn left through trees to reach parkland as in Section 2a.

3. Over stile, turn right onto driveway past WOODYARD COTTAGES (C) on RHS. Just past the cottages bear right up a grassy woodland path. Continue on path over several path junctions to meet a bridleway opposite a farmhouse.

4. Turn right along bridleway for about ¼ mile, then turn left at first path on left. Follow this path through woodland with field on LHS until it joins a bridleway leading to a clearing with road on RHS. Veer right just before next belt of trees to join bridleway to road. At a small group of trees on the opposite side of the road, cross over and pass bridleway post.

5. Follow path diagonally across large field to corner of wood and path junction. Turn right with wood on LHS and continue on path which twists and bends through mixed bracken and woodland. At junction with track turn left.

6. At next track junction bear left and follow this track as it bears right. Continue on track to road, ignoring paths to left and right.

7. Cross road and follow track as it bears left. Cross surfaced road and continue along bridleway (SP). At path junction bear right along edge of ridge, with views over ALDBURY (D) to left. Cross over first path junction, then when track joins from left continue ahead and slightly to right to return uphill to Bridgewater Monument. **1.1**

▼ WILSTONE RESERVOIR (WALKS 2 & 9)

▲ BERKHAMSTED CASTLE (WALK 4)

▼ DUDSWELL (WALK 5)

▲ ALDBURY (WALK 6)

WALK 9

LENGTH: 6 MILES
TIME: 3 HOURS

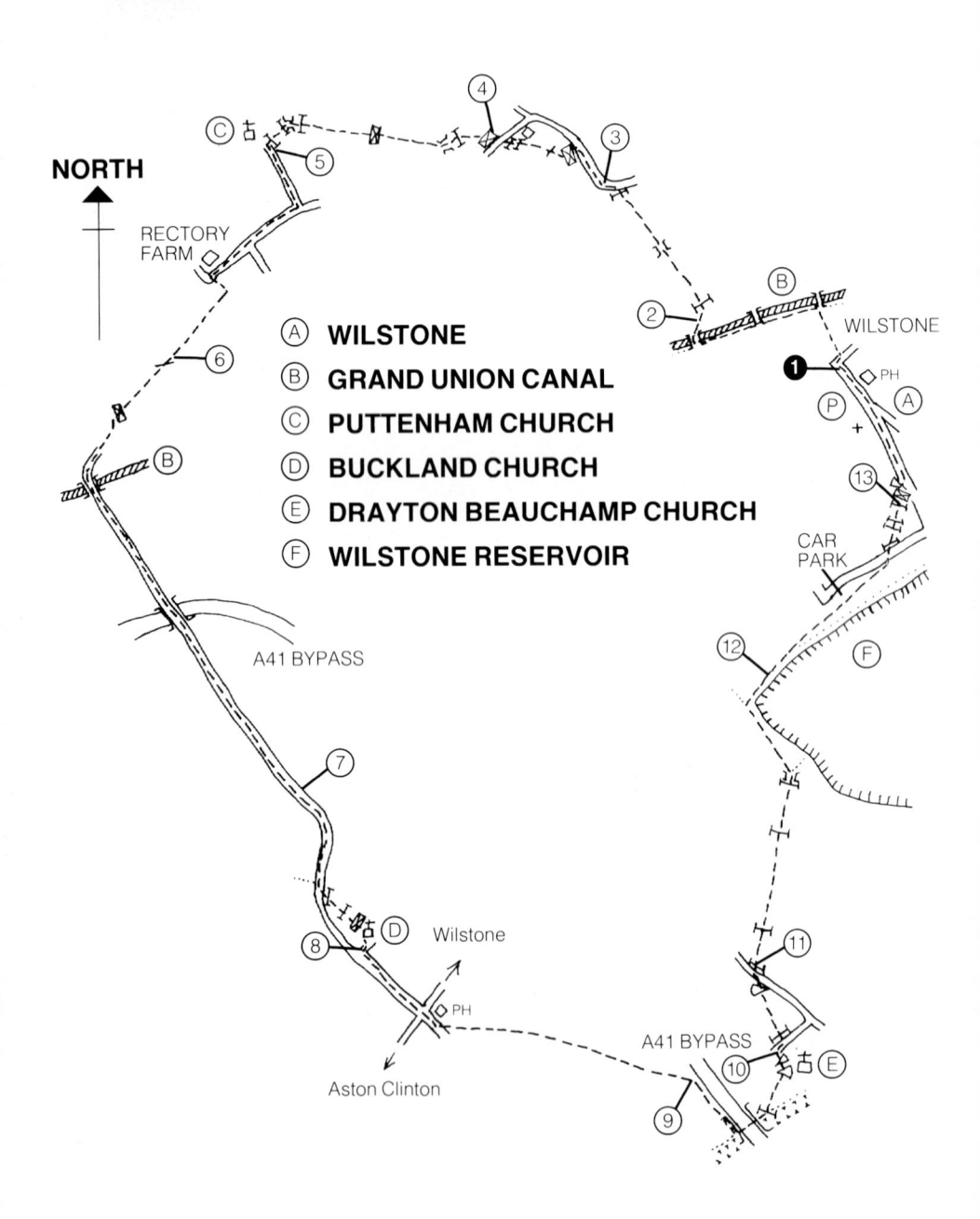

NORTH

- Ⓐ **WILSTONE**
- Ⓑ **GRAND UNION CANAL**
- Ⓒ **PUTTENHAM CHURCH**
- Ⓓ **BUCKLAND CHURCH**
- Ⓔ **DRAYTON BEAUCHAMP CHURCH**
- Ⓕ **WILSTONE RESERVOIR**

WILSTONE - PUTTENHAM - BUCKLAND

WALK 9

Park (P) in WILSTONE VILLAGE (A), near The Half Moon PH (GR SP904 141). The village has a limited bus service. Alternative parking is available beside WILSTONE RESERVOIR (GR SP903 134) : if parking here start the walk at Section 12. **45**

1. Facing PH turn left and follow road round to right. At SP turn left beside playing field to CANAL (B) and turn left along towpath. Continue past a lock and under bridge to second bridge. **23.1**

2. Cross bridge and then diagonally right across field to gap in hedge. Over wooden FB and stile, continue across open field with hedge on RHS to next FB. Keep to RHS of next field, then bear slightly left to stile onto road.

3. Turn left along road. After about 200 yards, turn left through gateway along unmarked path. Keep to RH edge of paddock, and at far RH corner cross wooden barriers into field. Cross field, with farm buildings on RHS, to two stiles across small enclosure at far corner. Over stiles to road.

4. Cross road and through gate opposite (SP). Cross field diagonally left to stile which leads footpath to small FB. Over this bear right across next two fields, the first to gate near farm and the second to double stile and FB leading towards church. Cross next field to stile adjoining PUTTENHAM CHURCH (C). **39.1**

5. Turn left to follow church access road to T junction. Turn right on road, and when road bends left continue straight on along farm track. When track bends right, cross fence into field ahead. Turn left and follow edge of field round first corner to far LH corner. Through gap in hedge continue along edge of next field.

6.* At next corner turn left over wooden barrier, then right into next field and continue along field edge to gate. Through gate turn left onto track and then right on lane. Cross bridge over canal and continue along lane, crossing bridge over bypass, to BUCKLAND village. **12**

7. Walk through village for about ¼ mile, until SP is seen on RHS. Do not turn right, but a few yards further on turn left over stile into field. Turn right along line of fence towards ALL SAINTS CHURCH (D). Cross stile into field adjoining churchyard, then go through gate into churchyard. A visit to the church is recommended. **12.1**

8. Leave churchyard via lych gate and turn right and then left onto road. Continue straight over crossroads, passing house and PH on LHS. At SP turn left and follow footpath diagonally across fields.

9.* Turn right and follow path along edge of A41 bypass to CANAL. Turn left under bypass, then take next path on left over stile. Bear right to kissing gate into churchyard of ST MARYS CHURCH (E), Drayton Beauchamp. **18**

10. Leave churchyard on access road, through two kissing gates, and bear round to right. At SP turn left over stile, cross field to far RH corner and go through kissing gate. Turn left along lane for 40 yards, then cross stile at SP on right.

11. Cross field to stile and go straight across next field to next stile/gate. WILSTONE RESERVOIR (F) can now be seen ahead. In next field continue on same line to far LH corner. A stile and FB leads into Nature Reserve. Bear left along edge of reserve to corner of reservoir, then turn right. **23.2**

12. Follow path on reservoir embankment to path down to car parking area. At the bottom of this path, continue along edge of embankment to SP on left across road. Take this path over stile and cross field diagonally right. Negotiate double wooden fence in middle of field.

13. At far RH corner cross stiles and FB. Over farm track go through wooden gate and cross corner of paddock to kissing gates with FB between. Turn left onto lane and continue into Wilstone village.

25

WALK 10

LENGTH: 4½ MILES
TIME: 2½ HOURS

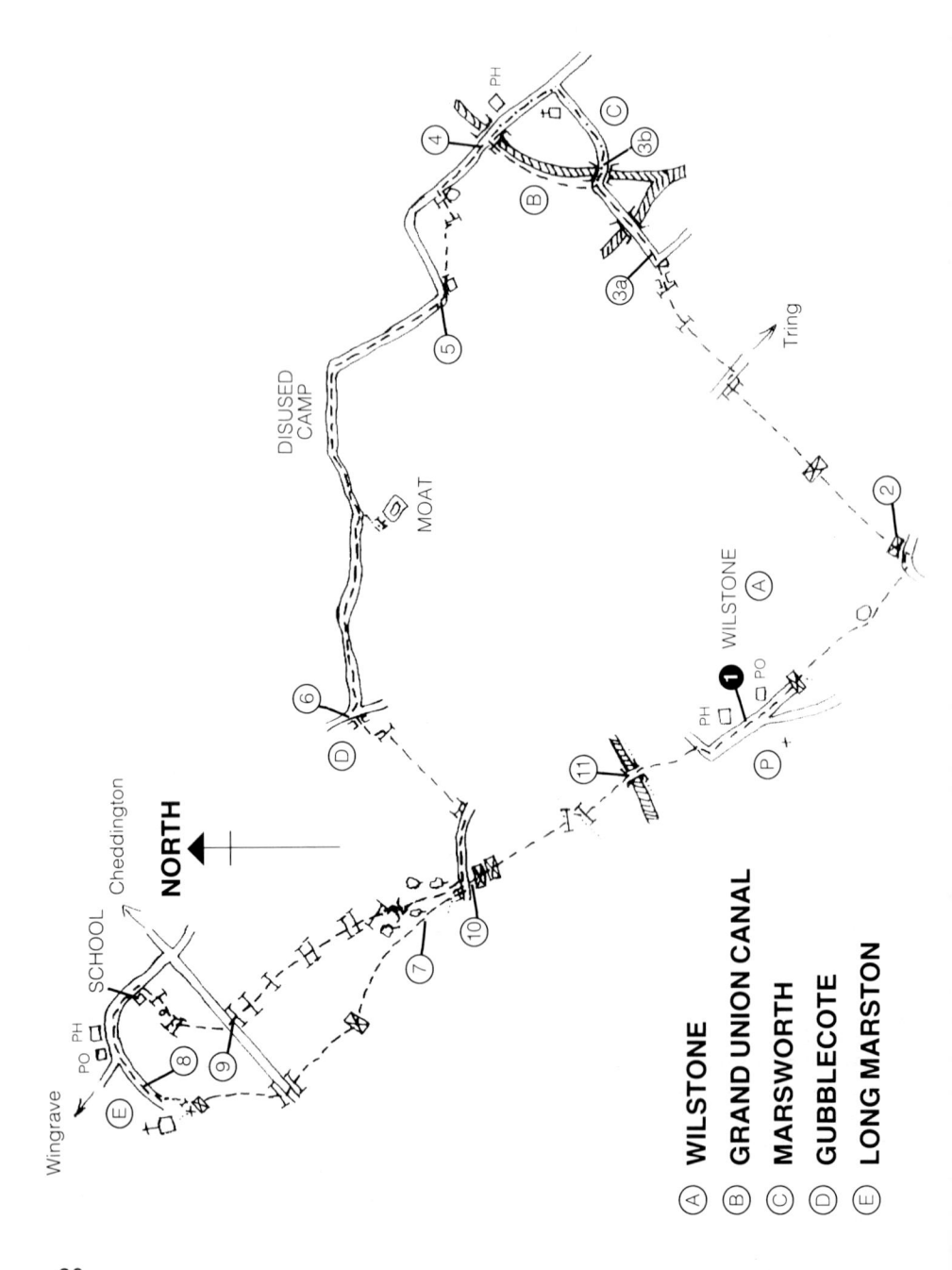

Ⓐ **WILSTONE**
Ⓑ **GRAND UNION CANAL**
Ⓒ **MARSWORTH**
Ⓓ **GUBBLECOTE**
Ⓔ **LONG MARSTON**

26

WILSTONE - MARSWORTH - LONG MARSTON **WALK 10**

Park in WILSTONE VILLAGE (A), near to Half Moon PH (P) (GR SP904 141). Limited bus services operate to Wilstone. **45**

1. Facing PH turn right, then fork left with bus shelter on RHS. Pass village Post Office/Stores on LHS, and follow cul-de-sac to end. Through gate, take farm track round pond and on to main road. Turn left on road and after a few yards turn left at SP onto track through gate into field.

2. Forward on path with hedge on LHS to gate in fence. Continue through next field to stile onto road. Turn right for a few yards then left at SP, keeping fence on LHS. Cross next stile and bear right to a stile opposite. Over stile and footbridge, through hedged alleyway to swing gate.

3a. Go straight on along road and over first canal bridge. Do not cross second bridge but turn left along towpath. Follow CANAL (B) to next bridge and turn left on road away from village. **23.1**

3b. To visit ALL SAINTS CHURCH and MARSWORTH village (C), continue over second bridge, turn left at T-junction, pass PH on RHS and rejoin walk at next canal bridge. **35.1**

4. Follow road to SP just after pond on LHS. Turn left over stile and bear right to next stile. Cross field diagonally right to far corner and over wooden barrier. Take narrow path between hedge and metal barn and cross next barrier onto road.

5. Turn left along road and continue for just over $1/2$ mile, passing a deserted camp on RHS and on LHS a field with earthworks and moat. These are the remains of a deserted mediaeval village, and may be visited by taking path at SP and crossing footbridge and stile on left.

6. Follow road to T-junction at GUBBLECOTE (D). Turn right, then left after about 20 yards over a wooden FB and down an alley between houses. Turn left at the bottom and after a few yards right over stile into corner of field. Cross field with hedge on LHS to stile/gate leading over FB onto road. Turn right on road for about 200 yards, then take stile on right into field (ignore path to RHS of stile). **33.1**

7. Keep to RH edge of field, cross the line of an old hedge and continue through gateway into next field. Continue with hedge on RHS to stile onto road. Over stile/gate opposite, cross field diagonally right towards the old Church of LONG MARSTON (E). Note ridge and furrow cultivation in this field. Through gate, cross FB and immediately over stile on right. Cross small field diagonally left and out onto road. **33.2**

8. Follow road round to right and into centre of village. Turn right, passing shop and PH on LHS, and continue to SP immediately after school on RHS. Take path between fence and hedge and over stile. Pass pond on RHS and cross pair of stiles into next field. Bear left across field to SP just before row of houses.

9. Cross road, over stile opposite and follow path over next stile. Continue with hedge on LHS, over stile, across next field to double stile and then across another field to double stile near RH corner. Over stile and FB, then after about 50 yards turn right over stile into woods. Follow path left to stream and over FB. Turn left along path to road.

10. Cross road and take path through two gates (SP). Straight on across field, keeping trees of old hedge on LHS. At far side of field locate stile ahead and slightly to left. Over this stile, then over next stile on left and cross field diagonally right to footbridge over canal.

11. Cross bridge and take path past playing field on RHS. Turn right on road and follow back into Wilstone village.

27

WALK 11

LENGTH: 8 MILES
TIME: 4 HOURS

- Ⓐ **BRIDGEWATER MONUMENT**
- Ⓑ **DUNCOMBE TERRACE**
- Ⓒ **INCOMBE HOLE**
- Ⓓ **IVINGHOE BEACON**
- Ⓔ **HANGING COOMBE**
- Ⓕ **RINGSHALL**
- Ⓖ **ASHRIDGE GOLF CLUBHOUSE**
- Ⓗ **ASHRIDGE COLLEGE**

Ivinghoe

CLIPPER DOWN COTTAGE

WARDS HURST FARM

Dagnall

B4506

NORTH

B4506

OLD PARK LODGE

Northchurch

28

BRIDGEWATER MONUMENT - IVINGHOE BEACON

WALK 11

Park (P) at the BRIDGEWATER MONUMENT (A) off B4506, main Northchurch - Ringshall road (GR SP970 131). A charge is made for parking at weekends. No regular public transport is available.

1. Walk up to MONUMENT and then turn right into trees on a wide path. Cross over wooden FB, pass tumulus on LHS and follow main track as it bears slightly left and passes a building on LHS. Continue through beechwoods on approximately the same contour. There are fine views to the left as track curves round to left at DUNCOMBE TERRACE (B). **4.1**

2. Ignore paths to left and right and continue to Clipper Down Cottage (boarding kennels on RHS). Through gate take track which bears right and then descends. Ignore track to left and continue for about ½ mile until track starts to rise. Take marked bridleway on left and cross over next path junction.

3. Emerge from woods to fine view along INCOMBE HOLE (C). Turn right along track: the next part of the walk follows the RIDGEWAY PATH (RP). At first gate on left, cross stile into field. Turn right and follow waymarked path through scrub thicket and down field. Cross stile on right and take path through open scrub, crossing a bank and ditch rampart. Over next stile follow track across road and on to IVINGHOE BEACON (D). **40** **27**

4. At top of hill turn right along the ridge and follow well defined grassy path to stile. The views are extensive, with Dunstable Downs ahead and Edlesborough church on a mound to the left. Continue to next stile, but do not cross it. Turn right and descend, with fence on LHS, over next stile/gate and on to junction with track. Turn right with fence on RHS, go through next gap and continue to next stile/gate with fence on LHS.

5. Over stile bear left, keeping belt of trees on LHS. Just below line of beech trees, cross stile into woods on well-defined path. Continue through wood and follow marker arrows ahead through conifer plantation. Emerge from wood with field on LHS and follow path straight ahead up steep hill (HANGING COOMBE (E).

6. Cross stile at top into small field, and cross diagonally right into farmyard. Turn left between farm and other buildings, then turn right into field and bear left to gate at far corner. Go straight on through three further gates and round the edge of Ringshall Coppice to stile. Cross grass with reservoir on RHS and turn right along concrete path. Continue over stile to road.

7. Turn left along road to RINGSHALL VILLAGE (F). At T-junction turn right, then left at double SP. Go through kissing gate and follow fence on LHS as it bears left. Cross stile in trees onto path leading to track and then tarmac road.

8. After about ½ mile there is a path on the left between larchlap and wire fences. To visit the Bridgewater Arms PH at LITTLE GADDESDEN take this path and return the same way. Take path opposite which crosses another private road and goes down a narrow alley with posts at each end. Continue into wood, across a golf tee and into another wood. Emerge between gardens onto drive and then road. **31.3**

9. Turn right and immediately left on road towards ASHRIDGE GOLF CLUBHOUSE (G). Just before clubhouse turn right onto grass, then left downhill and across small valley to wide track into trees. Beyond trees track doglegs round Old Park Lodge on RHS (Note sundials on walls). As track becomes road, continue past golf green on RHS to wide avenue with ASHRIDGE COLLEGE (H) to left. **4.3**

10. Turn right along avenue towards Bridgewater Monument. Go through gate, cross road and return to car park.

WALK 12

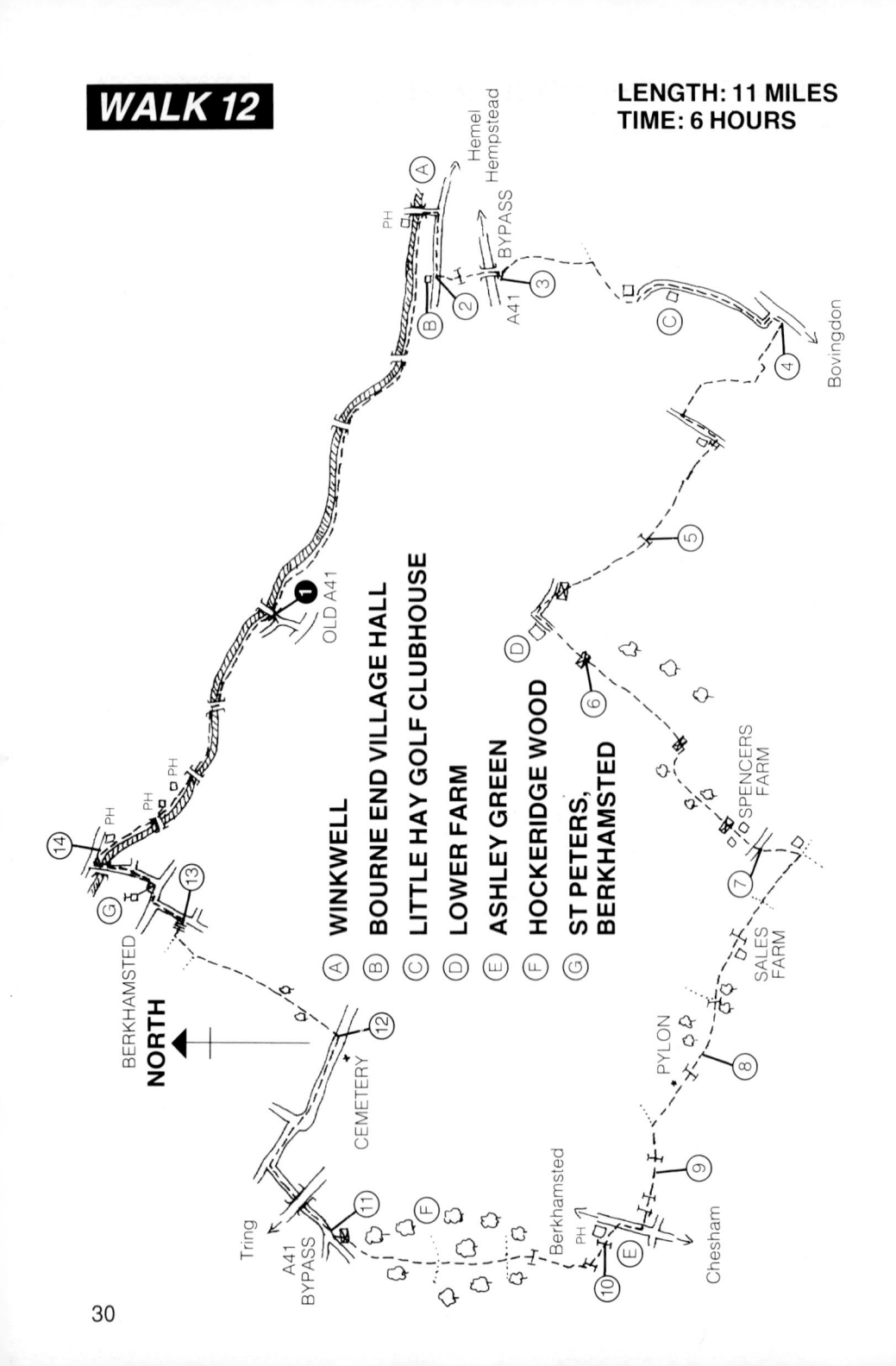

LENGTH: 11 MILES
TIME: 6 HOURS

- Ⓐ WINKWELL
- Ⓑ BOURNE END VILLAGE HALL
- Ⓒ LITTLE HAY GOLF CLUBHOUSE
- Ⓓ LOWER FARM
- Ⓔ ASHLEY GREEN
- Ⓕ HOCKERIDGE WOOD
- Ⓖ ST PETERS, BERKHAMSTED

BERKHAMSTED - BOURNE END - ASHLEY GREEN WALK 12

Park (P) at junction of Bulbeggars Lane and Bank Mill Lane (GR TL006 071). Buses pass nearby on old A41.

1. Turn away from old A41 along Bulbeggars Lane. Where road bears right to canal bridge, take path to left onto towpath. Turn right under bridge and follow towpath for about 1½ miles, passing four locks and going under two bridges. At swing bridge near The Three Horseshoes PH, turn right up WINKWELL (A). Turn right along main road. **46**

2.* Just before BOURNE END Village Hall (B) on RHS, cross road to track between houses. Follow track over stile and beside hedge on RHS to bridge over A41 bypass. Cross bridge, turn right alongside bypass and then left on footpath. **8**

3. Bear left across golf course to SP, then turn right up hill. Pass another SP and at SP at top of hill turn right. Follow path along top of golf course, past houses on LHS, to barns. Turn left onto road, which curves round to right and passes LITTLE HAY GOLF CLUB HOUSE (C) on RHS. Continue on road to Golf Complex entrance. **32**

4. Just within gateway turn right at bridleway SP. Follow this path as it skirts golf course on RHS for about ½ mile. Turn left along lane. At SP just after two houses on RHS turn right over stile. Continue to corner of field with hedge on RHS, then take small path through hedgerow and turn left along edge of next field.

5. At next corner locate stile slightly uphill. Cross into next field and bear right on path across field, eventually meeting hedge and following this on LHS down to gate. Turn left along farm track and follow round to left, passing LOWER FARM (D) on RHS.

6. Continue through gate and then on path up the middle of field with wood to LHS. Through further gate, turn right along field edge. As trees end at top of path, continue across open field to tree lined track. Follow through gate and between farm buildings to road.

7. Cross road and take track at SP. Just beyond farm buildings on LHS, turn right on unmarked footpath heading straight across field to stile. Continue past Sales Farm on LHS and along a hedged path. When path bends to right and widens, cross stile on left and cross field diagonally left, passing trees on RHS.

8. Keep heading towards large electricity pylon in next field, and cross stile at bottom of hill. Follow path up field, pylon on RHS, until path reaches field corner. Keep on with fence on LHS to path junction. Turn left through gap and walk up RH field edge and over stile.

9. Continue on narrow path between fences to stile into grassy area. Go straight on to gate, over stile and along track to ASHLEY GREEN (E). Turn right on grass verge and cross road to car park of The Golden Eagle PH. **3**

10.* Cross stile at rear of car park. Take path across field to stile in far corner, then turn right along RH edge of next field. Follow path down to stile into HOCKERIDGE WOOD (F). Continue on path uphill in wood and follow main track ahead, ignoring paths to left and right, to gate onto road. **26**

11.* Turn right on lane and pass under A41 bypass bridge. At crossroads at top of hill, cross over and turn right on pavement. At next major junction cross road onto footpath opposite and continue along Kingshill Way.

12.* Just past cemetery on RHS, turn left through gap in fence into school playing fields. Follow FP along line of trees between pitches and then down alleyway. Continue to public sports field and keep on with allotments on RHS. At path junction turn right to steps down to road.

13. Cross Chesham Road and turn left to BERKHAMSTED High Street. Cross over pelican crossing, then turn right and then left onto cobbles. Go up steps on right to pass behind ST PETERS CHURCH (G). Go down next steps and turn left along Castle Street, passing Berkhamsted School on LHS. **7**

7.5

14. Over canal bridge turn right, and join canal towpath at The Crystal Palace PH. Follow towpath past two locks and under two bridges. At the third bridge the towpath rises to road. Cross canal and rejoin towpath under bridge. Continue past another lock and at next bridge take path to right onto road and return to car parking area.

WALK 13

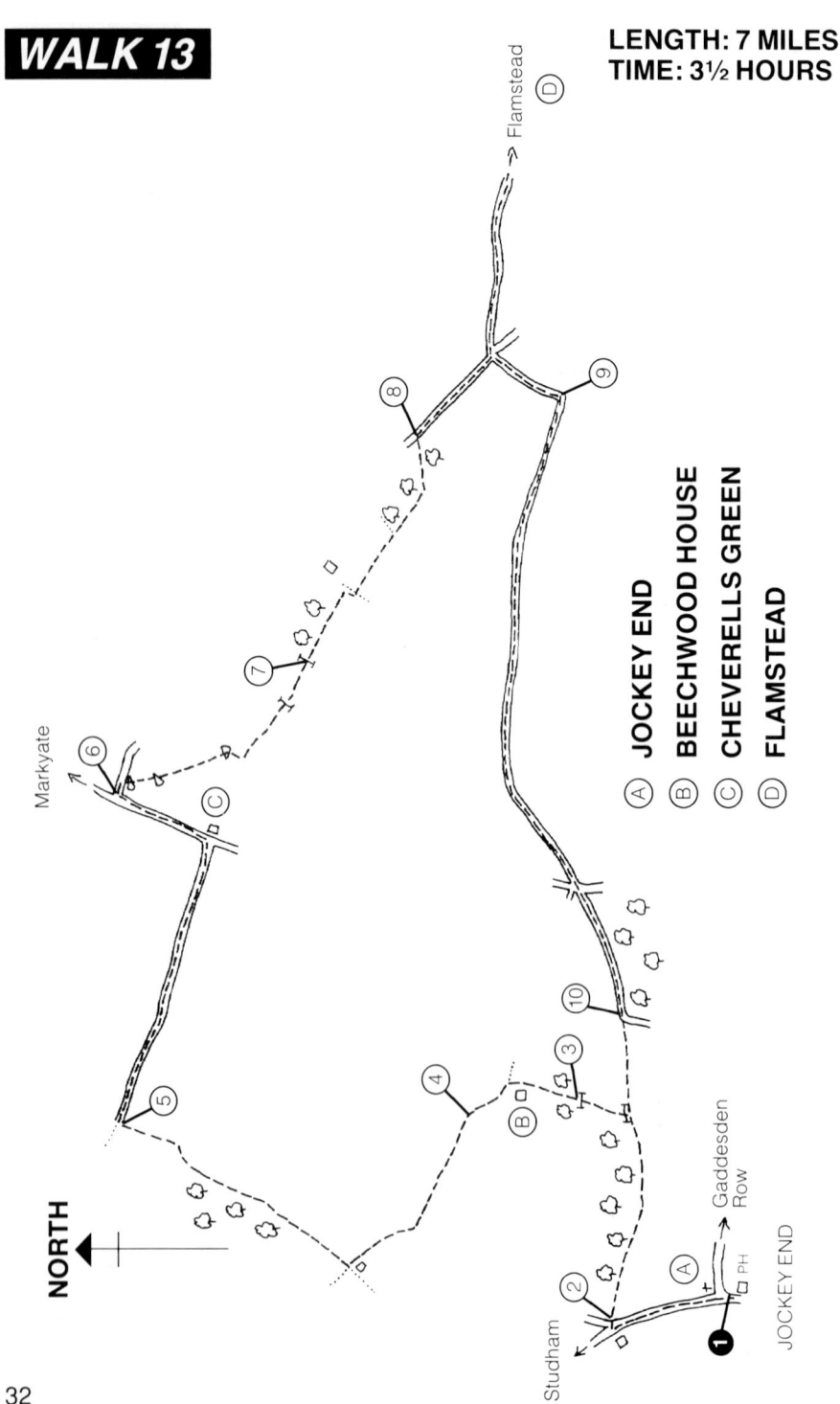

LENGTH: 7 MILES
TIME: 3½ HOURS

- Ⓐ JOCKEY END
- Ⓑ BEECHWOOD HOUSE
- Ⓒ CHEVERELLS GREEN
- Ⓓ FLAMSTEAD

32

JOCKEY END - FLAMSTEAD   *WALK 13*

Park in front of THE PLOUGH (P) at JOCKEY END (A) (GR TL 040137). **28**
There is a limited bus service.

1. Walk along grass verge beside road to Studham for about 300 yards, to road on right at bend opposite farm ('Private Road' sign ahead).
2. Turn right along bridleway (SP). Follow this wide track, which can be muddy underfoot, with woods on LHS and hedge on RHS for about ½ mile. At field on left cross stile and bear right up hill to stile into wood.
3. Go straight ahead through wood, skirting to right of central group of trees, and emerge at the back of BEECHWOOD HOUSE (B), which is a school. **6** Bear right and skirt the buildings, with boundary wall on LHS and playing fields on RHS. Through car park, turn left onto tarmac road and pass in front of school.
4. Continue on unsurfaced road for about ½ mile, passing 'Private Road' sign. At crossroads (Kennels Lodge) turn right. Keep on for another ½ mile, with pleasant woods on LHS.
5. When track meets road, turn right and continue through Roe Green to CHEVERELLS GREEN (C). At road junction with large old house (Cheverells) opposite, turn left along wide grass verge and walk beside road to turning on right (SP Flamstead).
6. Cross the road and walk down lane for about 30 yards. Turn right at SP through kissing gate and cross field diagonally to second kissing gate. Follow fence on RHS to another kissing gate, then turn right along field edge to corner and continue to stile. Take path ahead bearing slightly left to stile.
7. Over stile follow field edge with wood on LHS. At far side of field turn right to SP, then left along field edge with plantation, then hedge on LHS. Do not turn left at corner of wood but continue with wood on LHS to SP. Take path through the wood to road.
8. Turn right on road for about ¼ mile to crossroads. To visit FLAMSTEAD (D) **20** turn left for about ½ mile and then retrace steps. To continue walk turn right (SP Hemel Hempstead).
9. At foot of slight hill turn sharp right on road. Continue for about ¼ mile to road junction and entrance to Beechwood Park School. Cross to lane opposite (to left of school entrance) and follow lane for about ¼ mile, until it bends to left.
10. Take wide bridleway ahead (blocked to traffic) and continue for ½ mile to road. Turn left and retrace steps to Jockey End.

WALK 14

LENGTH: 5 MILES
TIME: 2½ HOURS

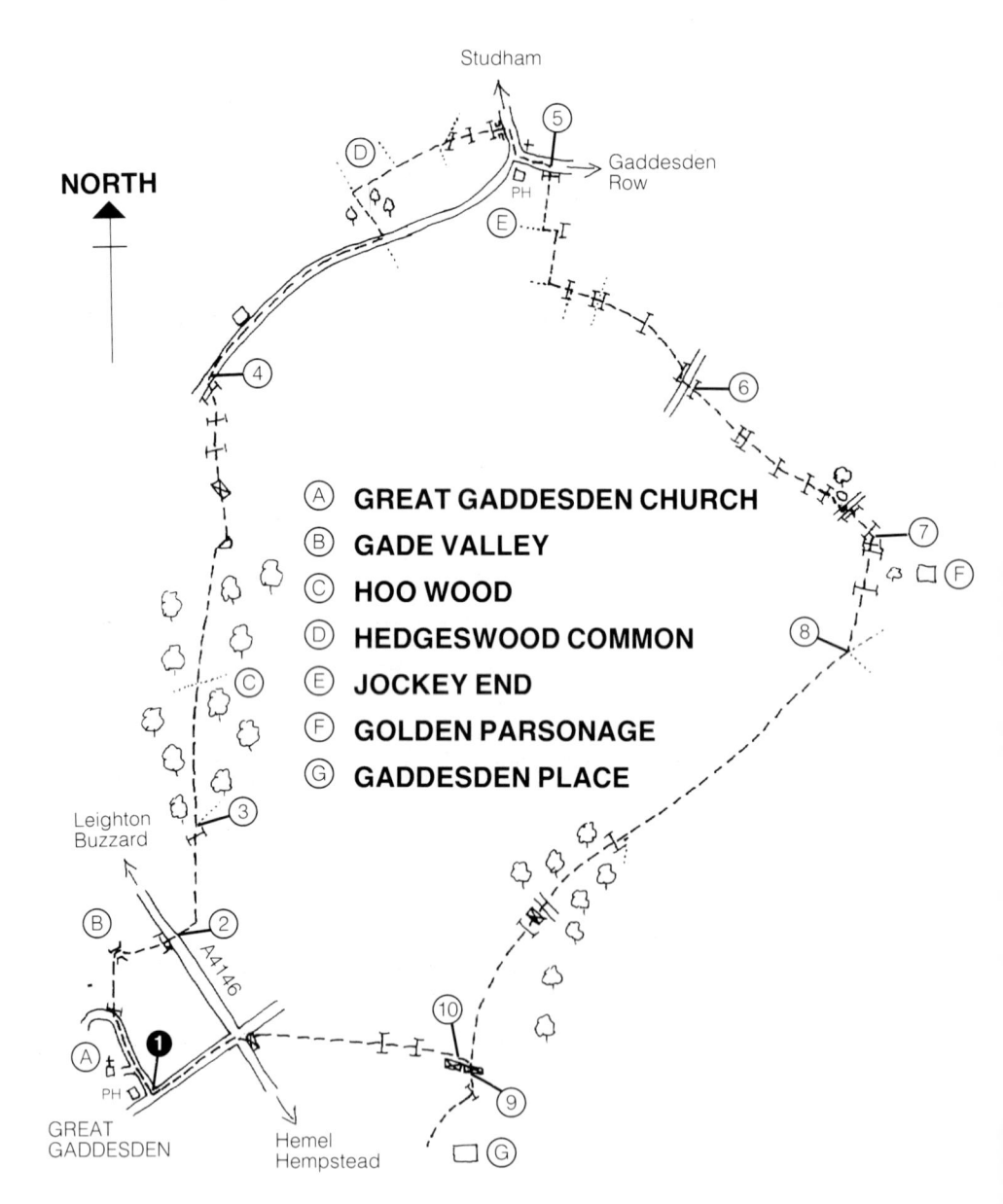

NORTH

- (A) **GREAT GADDESDEN CHURCH**
- (B) **GADE VALLEY**
- (C) **HOO WOOD**
- (D) **HEDGESWOOD COMMON**
- (E) **JOCKEY END**
- (F) **GOLDEN PARSONAGE**
- (G) **GADDESDEN PLACE**

Studham
Gaddesden Row
Leighton Buzzard
A4146
GREAT GADDESDEN
Hemel Hempstead

34

GREAT GADDESDEN - JOCKEY END *WALK 14*

Park (P) in GREAT GADDESDEN village (A), near The Cock and Bottle PH (GR TL029 112). The village has a limited bus service.

1. Walk along cul-de-sac with open ground on RHS and turning to CHURCH (A) on LHS. Pass school, then houses on LHS, and when road bends to left cross stile on right at edge of play area. Turn left and cross field to gap in hedge, then follow path as it curves right to footbridge over course of River Gade. Continue across meadow to stile onto road.

2. Cross the road and take concrete path at SP between houses and village hall. Path goes up hill at edge of field and veers left with hedge on RHS. When hedge bends right, path runs straight ahead across open field to HOO WOOD (C). Note views to left of GADE VALLEY (B). Locate stile into wood about 40 yards uphill from corner.

3. On entering wood take left track at fork. Continue on this track and go straight on at path junction. Path runs slightly downhill and presently a field can be seen on LHS. Turn left through kissing gate. Follow RH edge of field down to gateway, turn left into next field and walk uphill with hedge on LHS. Cross stile and continue to further stile, then on with hedge on RHS to stile onto road.

4. Turn right along lane, past farm on LHS, to SP on left. Take this path onto HEDGESWOOD COMMON (D). Pass between scrub area on RHS and newly-planted area on LHS, then after 150 yards turn right across Common to meet corner of field. Continue with hedge on LHS to corner of Common. Cross stile between hedges to right of farm track and cross field with hedge on LHS to next stile. Continue along edge of next field to stile and cross FB to road. Turn right along road to SP about 100 yards past THE PLOUGH PH (E).

5. Turn right over stile and follow path with hedge on LHS. Turn left at path junction and at next stile do not cross but turn right with hedge on LHS. Follow hedge as it bends left, and over next stile take path straight ahead. Path crosses farm track with stiles each side and continues straight across field. Over next stile follow fence across field. Turn right along hedge and left over stile into lane.

6. Cross stile opposite and follow line of SP across field. Cross pair of stiles in wide hedge, then continue to another stile. Over this bear slightly left to next stile, then cross paddock to stile in LH corner. Skirt round pond to lane, turn left and then right over stile at SP.

7. At corner of field cross stile and then pair of stiles into field on left. Follow path diagonally right, passing trees on LHS with GOLDEN PARSONAGE (F) beyond, to stile over wire fence and then on to gap in fence onto track.

8. Turn right along track for about ½ mile to a stile into Marsh Wood. Follow track through wood, then cross farm road to gate ahead. Go through gate and over another stile into field. Walk on down field with wood to LHS to double gateway. Note views of the Gade Valley and Great Gaddesden to right.

9. To see GADDESDEN PLACE (G) and get still better views, go through left gate and after a few yards right over stile. Cross field towards a second stile. Retrace steps to end of Section 8.

10. Turn downhill with fence on LHS. Follow path over two stiles, then across a large field down to a gate onto main road. Cross over and take road opposite down to Great Gaddesden.

22
22.1
22.2
28
22.3
22.5

WALK 15

LENGTH: 5 MILES
TIME: 2½ HOURS

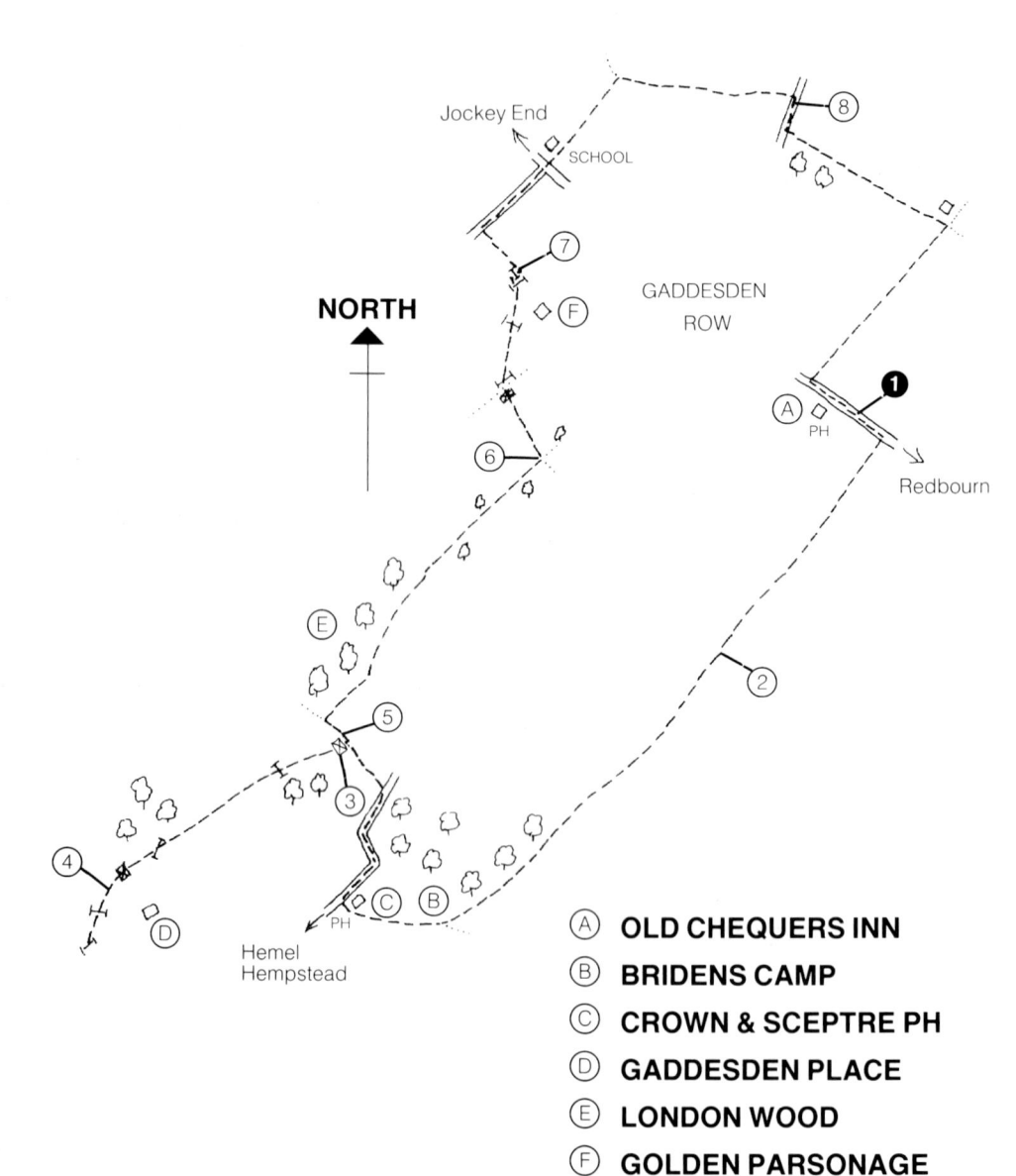

- Ⓐ **OLD CHEQUERS INN**
- Ⓑ **BRIDENS CAMP**
- Ⓒ **CROWN & SCEPTRE PH**
- Ⓓ **GADDESDEN PLACE**
- Ⓔ **LONDON WOOD**
- Ⓕ **GOLDEN PARSONAGE**

GADDESDEN ROW - BRIDEN'S CAMP

WALK 15

Park near THE OLD CHEQUERS INN (A) in Gaddesden Row (GR TL057 123). Occasional buses stop about ¼ mile towards Jockey End.

1. From PH turn right along grass verge beside road to Redbourn. After 200 yards turn right at SP to Briden's Camp. Take path with hedge on LHS to gap in hedge which leads through to farm track.
2. With hedge now on RHS continue on track to Big Wood. Follow path with wood on RHS until it veers right to an opening onto farm track. This area is known as BRIDEN'S CAMP (B). Turn right and follow to road at the CROWN AND SCEPTRE PH (C). Turn right along road for ¼ mile until a track turns left (SP Great Gaddesden). Follow track for 200 yards to gateway on left. **11**
3. To see Gaddesden Place, turn left through gateway. Follow path ahead, which bears right with wood on LHS to another stile. Take path diagonally right across next field to stile with another wood on RHS. Turn left over stile and with fence on LHS cross field towards a gate set slightly to the right ahead.
4. Cross field to a stile just to the left ahead and follow across next field to another stile. There are good views of the Gade Valley and Great Gaddesden to the right, and to the left is GADDESDEN PLACE (D). Retrace steps to end of Section 2. **22.5**
5. Carry on along farm track for 100 yards, to SP at the edge of LONDON WOOD (E). Turn right and follow path with wood on LHS. When wood ends, turn left and right to continue along an avenue of trees to a dip and path junction.
6. Turn left and at top of field go through gateway onto farm track and turn right. Almost immediately on the left cross another stile (or pass through gap). Cross field diagonally right, over stile across fence and on to double stile in corner of field. Note the GOLDEN PARSONAGE (F) across field to right. **22.3**
7. Over double stile turn right over another stile, then turn left along field edge to private road. Turn right and walk up to road. Cross over and follow track opposite, with school on LHS. At junction with next track turn right and walk on with hedge on RHS to road.
8. Turn right and then after about 100 yards left at bridleway SP. Follow track with hedge on RHS to farm, then turn right down farm track to road and return to the Old Chequers Inn.

37

WALK 16

LENGTH: 5 MILES
TIME: 2½ HOURS

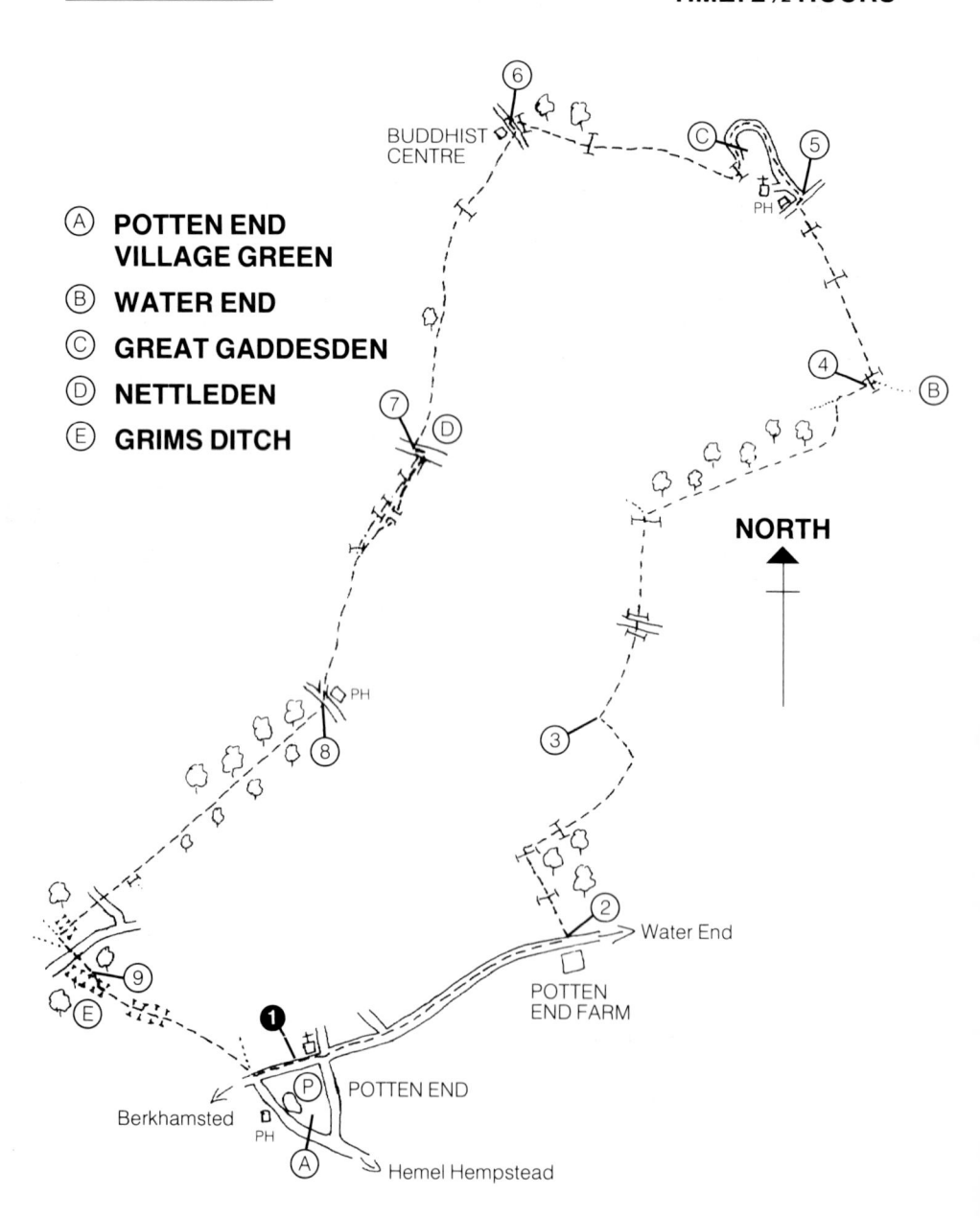

- Ⓐ **POTTEN END VILLAGE GREEN**
- Ⓑ **WATER END**
- Ⓒ **GREAT GADDESDEN**
- Ⓓ **NETTLEDEN**
- Ⓔ **GRIMS DITCH**

POTTEN END - GREAT GADDESDEN - NETTLEDEN

WALK 16

Park (P) on POTTEN END VILLAGE GREEN (A) opposite village hall (GR TL017 088). The village has a good bus service (not Sundays).   **38.1**

1. Facing village hall turn right and walk along pavement for about ½ mile, passing garage on RHS.
2. Opposite Potten End Farm on RHS turn left at SP to Great Gaddesden. After one stile the path continues downhill to second stile. Over this turn right and follow path with wood on RHS. Continue over next stile and along field edge with hedge on RHS. At end of hedge turn left on clear path.
3. At marker post 150 yards from farm buildings turn right across field down to stile onto road. Cross stile opposite and follow path uphill to stile into wood. At fork in wood take right path, with field close on RHS. Path continues through wood and eventually runs downhill, then bears left to a T-junction. Turn right down hill with hedge on LHS.
4. At pair of stiles it is possible to detour to visit WATER END (B), by bearing right and across River Gade. Otherwise turn left over stiles and take path along bottom of field. Continue to stile, then between hedge and fence over another stile and on into GREAT GADDESDEN (C).   **22.4**
5. Cross road and walk along minor road with open space on RHS, passing turning to church on LHS. Follow road past school and then houses on LHS and then around curve to left to reach row of garages. Cross forecourt to stile at left of garages. Over stile cross field diagonally right uphill to a gap in hedge. Continue on same line across next field to corner of woods. Cross stile and follow path with wood on RHS to stile onto road.
6. Turn left along road for 50 yards, then right at SP by entrance to Amaravati Buddhist Centre. Follow path over stile with hedges on both sides. Continue into field and on down hill with hedge on LHS to NETTLEDEN (D).   **38.2**
7. Turn left on road and after a few yards right up sunken lane. Either continue up lane or take path on RHS at SP over stile. Path goes up hill with hedge on LHS, crossing two stiles partway up and then another into lane at top. Follow the lane down hill to Alford Arms PH.
8. From PH take footpath opposite (SP) into trees. After nearly ½ mile, pass stile on LHS and go straight over private road and through wooden barrier. Follow path through another barrier and across ditch, then turn left onto wider path leading down to road.
9. Take path straight ahead, which bears round to right to join GRIMS DITCH (E). Follow ditch across golf course into trees, then onto path with gardens on LHS. Bear round to right and turn left on road to return to Potten End. NB Grims Ditch can be very muddy, but there are several other paths following similar direction.   **24**

▼ BERKHAMSTED SCHOOL (WALK 12)

▼ WINKWELL (WALKS 12, 20 & 32)

▼ BRIDGEWATER MONUMENT (WALKS 6, 8 & 11)

▲ PUTTENHAM CHURCH (WALK 9)

▼ GOLDEN PARSONAGE (WALKS 14 & 15)

▲ GADDESDEN PLACE (WALKS 14 & 15)

▼ NETTLEDEN (WALK 16)

▲ POTTEN END (WALKS 16 & 18)

41

WALK 17

LENGTH: 6½ MILES or 6 MILES
TIME: 3 HOURS

- (A) **MARKYATE**
- (B) **PEPPERSTOCK**
- (C) **OLD WATLING ST**
- (D) **FLAMSTEAD**

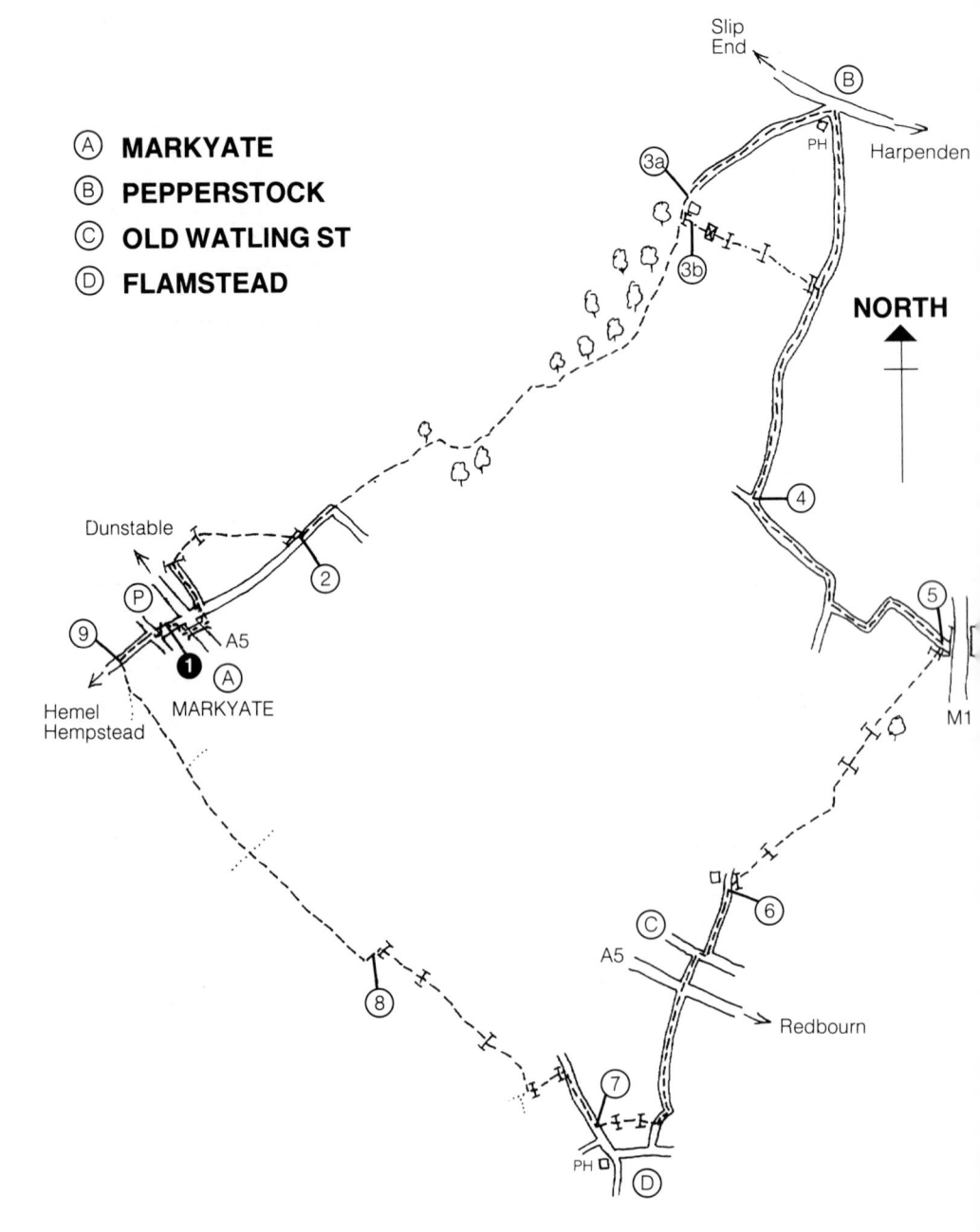

NORTH

MARKYATE - PEPPERSTOCK - FLAMSTEAD   WALK 17

Park in centre of MARKYATE (A) in Hicks Road Car Park (P) (GR TL062 163). There is a good bus service to Markyate.

1. Turn left from the car park towards the A5 and cross over footbridge. Cross Hicks Road and walk up The Ridings. At end of the road cross stile, turn right and follow hedge on RHS to next stile. Cross into next field and take path diagonally right to gate/stile in far corner.

2. Turn left along lane until it bends to right. Go straight ahead on track, known as Half Moon Lane. Follow this track for about a mile until it opens out with houses on RHS.

3a. To visit PEPPERSTOCK (B) continue ahead into village. Turn right at PH and walk down quiet lane (Pepsal End Road) for about ¾ mile to junction.

3b. Alternatively, turn right over stile just before houses. Take path between enclosure on RHS and sheds on LHS and follow through gate and over two further stiles/gates. Bear slightly right across field to gate/stile onto lane. Turn right along lane and continue to junction.

4. Turn left at lane junction, then about ¼ mile further on turn left at next junction (SP Kinsbourne Green and Harpenden). Continue almost to M1 motorway bridge.

5. About 20 yards before bridge turn right over stile at SP. Take path with fence and then wood on LHS, and continue downhill beside fence to stile. Cross stile and follow path along edge of field and over next stile. Keep hedge on LHS and continue to stile onto road.

6. Turn left downhill to T-junction and turn right along OLD WATLING STREET (C). Turn left down lane and cross busy main road (A5). Continue up lane opposite into FLAMSTEAD (D). After first houses on LHS turn right at SP, past Lavender Cottage and over stile into field. Keep to LH field edge, then cross stile and walk down narrow alley.

7. Turn right along Hollybush Lane. After about 250 yards turn left over stile at SP. Bear slightly left to SP and stile on far side of field. Over stile turn right between hedge and wire fence, then over stile take path along RH field edge. Continue over two stiles, then over third stile turn left.

8. Follow hedge on LHS for about 75 yards, then turn right across large open field. Go straight on at path junction. When path is joined by hedge on RHS continue to corner of field. Follow path which bears right downhill to road.

9. Turn right along road, then at T-junction right and immediately left into Hicks Road and car park.

WALK 18

LENGTH: 3½ MILES
TIME: 2 HOURS

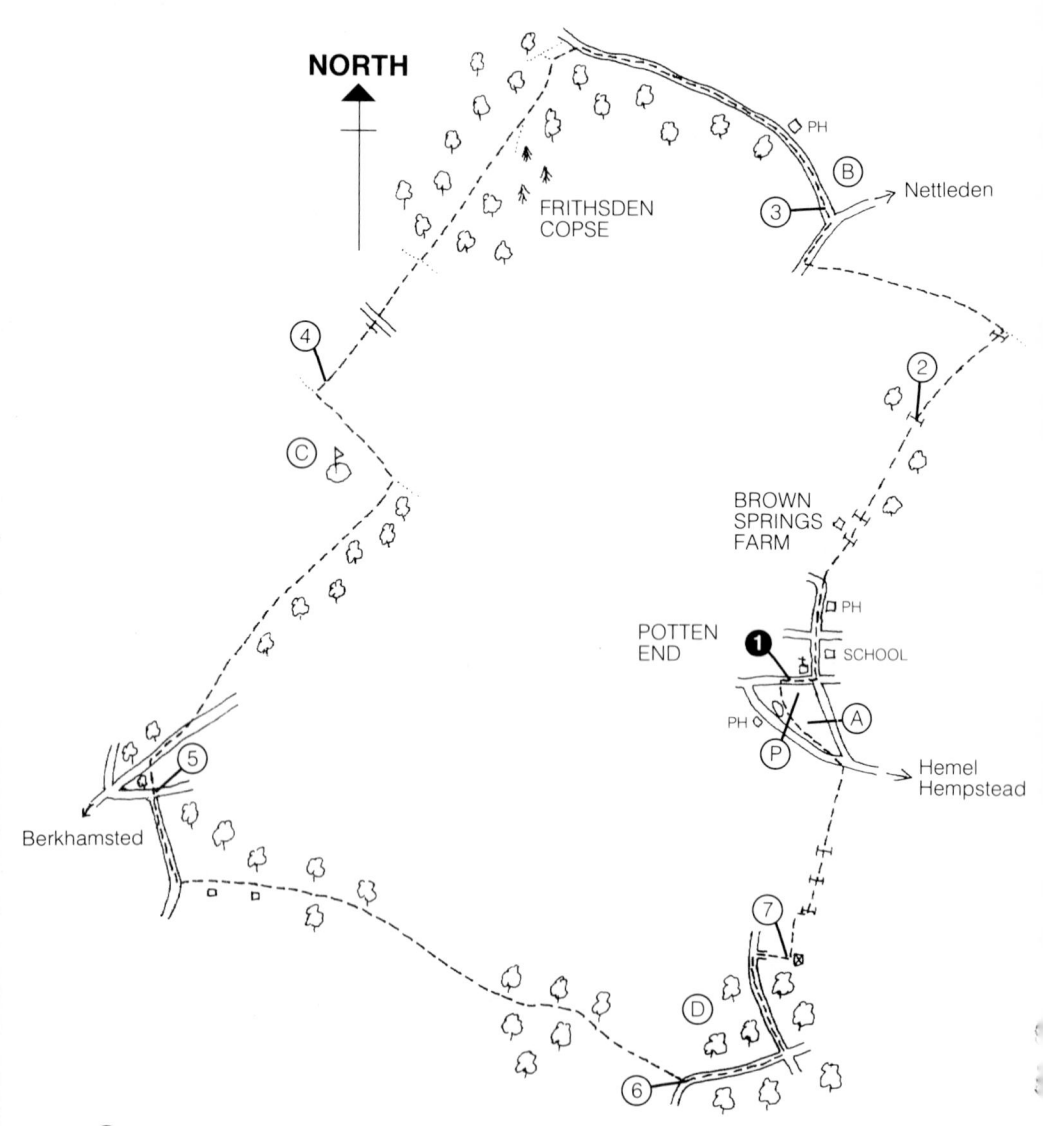

- Ⓐ **POTTEN END VILLAGE GREEN**
- Ⓑ **FRITHSDEN VINEYARD**
- Ⓒ **BERKHAMSTED GOLF COURSE**
- Ⓓ **LITTLE HEATH**

POTTEN END - FRITHSDEN COPSE *WALK 18*

38

Park (P) on POTTEN END VILLAGE GREEN (A) opposite village hall (GR TL017 088). The village has a good bus service (not Sundays).

1. Facing village hall turn right on pavement for about 100 yards. Turn left on road between church and school, and go straight on at crossroads. Pass The Plough PH on RHS and continue along farm track ahead (SP Nettleden Road). Cross two stiles at entrance to Brown Springs Farm and follow edge of field ahead with hedge on RHS.

2. Over next stile follow path across field to stile opposite. Turn left along bridleway. Note vineyard (B) on far RHS of valley. Turn right on lane, then left at junction (SP Frithsden & Ashridge).

3. Walk along lane for 1/3 mile, passing Alford Arms PH on RHS, then turn left at SP to Berkhamsted Common. Ignore first path to right, which links with parallel track, but about 100 yards up hill bear right at fork. Follow path through trees, then over path junction and on between fence and hedge. Cross private road and continue through wooden barrier opposite.

4. Emerge onto golf course (C) and after a few yards turn left on bridleway path. Before entering trees turn right and follow paths along edge of golf course. When golf course meets road on LHS, turn right along road. A few yards before 'Give Way' sign turn left on narrow path for a short distance to another road.

5. Straight ahead is a lane with SP to Gutteridge Farm. This is Ivy House Lane. Cross road and walk down lane for 200 yards. Turn left along unsurfaced road with houses on RHS. At end of road go straight on, following path which bears right through trees. Continue downhill between fences, with field on RHS, then on uphill through trees. At top of hill path follows field edge ahead with hedge on LHS.

6. Turn left on lane into LITTLE HEATH (D), then at crossroads turn left again. After about 200 yards turn right on wide shingled drive to Bulbeggars. Just before gateway into private house, turn left on narrow path between tall hedges.

7. Follow path round to right, then left over stile along path between paddocks. Continue between fences/hedges over two more stiles and straight on along surfaced drive. Turn left on road to return to Potten End Village Green.

45

WALK 19

LENGTH: 3½ MILES
TIME: 1½ HOURS

NORTH

WOOD FARM

Leighton Buzzard

Redbourn

HEMEL HEMPSTEAD OLD TOWN

Hemel Hempstead New Town

Ⓐ **OLD TOWN HIGH STREET**
Ⓑ **PICCOTTS END**

46

HEMEL HEMPSTEAD OLD TOWN - PICCOTTS END   WALK 19

Park in the large car park (P) at the end of the OLD TOWN HIGH STREET (A) (GR TL054 080). There are frequent buses to the Old Town.   25.2

1. From the car park turn away from St Mary's Church and along the road towards Piccotts End. Go straight ahead at roundabout, passing Marchmont Arms PH and then Boar's Head PH on LHS. Shortly after entering PICCOTTS END (B) there is a row of cottages on RHS, one of which contains mediaeval wall paintings. Continue along road to turning along Dodds Lane on RHS.   37

2. Walk up lane for ¼ mile, then turn left at SP and take track into field. Follow track as it turns right across field and goes through gap in hedges at corner of next field. Go straight on uphill with hedge on RHS to stile.

3. Over stile continue towards Wood Farm and cross stile into farm road. Turn right through farm buildings and follow road round bends to T-junction. Turn right for 150 yards, then left on path up steps at SP.

4. Follow path along field edge with hedge on RHS. In corner of field pass through gap in hedge and follow path left along side of field. With hedge on LHS continue uphill and bear right as path heads towards houses. Turn right along field edge, with houses on LHS, and continue round bends and away from houses to lane. Turn right and walk down hill to gate at bottom of lane.

5. After 100 yards turn left at SP to Hemel Hempstead and Cupid Green. Go through gate ahead and follow gravel track through car park, then round to right and up to gate/stile onto road. Cross road and take track ahead, passing tree plantation on LHS. Continue across field to SP and gap in hedge onto another road.

6. Cross road, turn downhill for a few yards then turn left. Walk along top edge of open grass area. At far end turn right down steps. Follow path into cul-de-sac and on down to Old High Street. Straight across High Street is the car park entrance.

47

WALKS IN

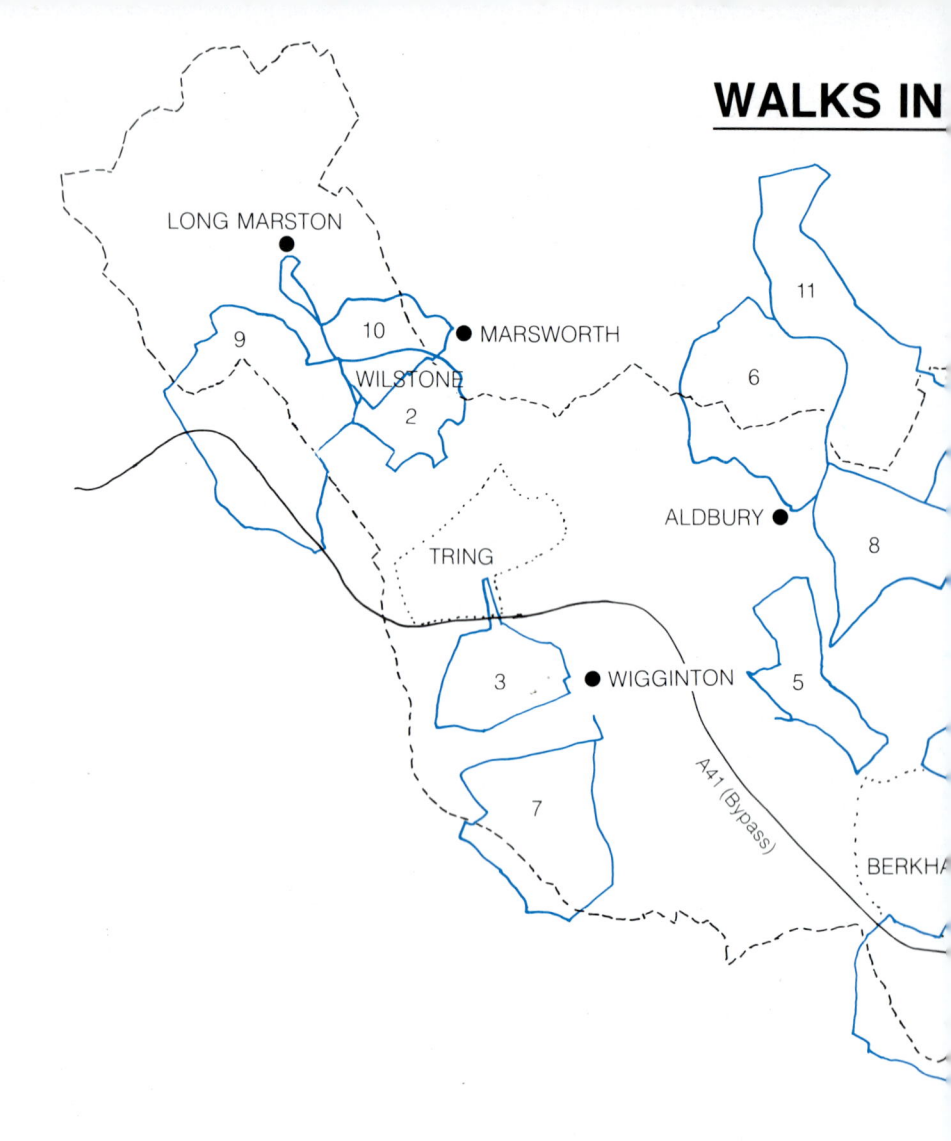

DACORUM

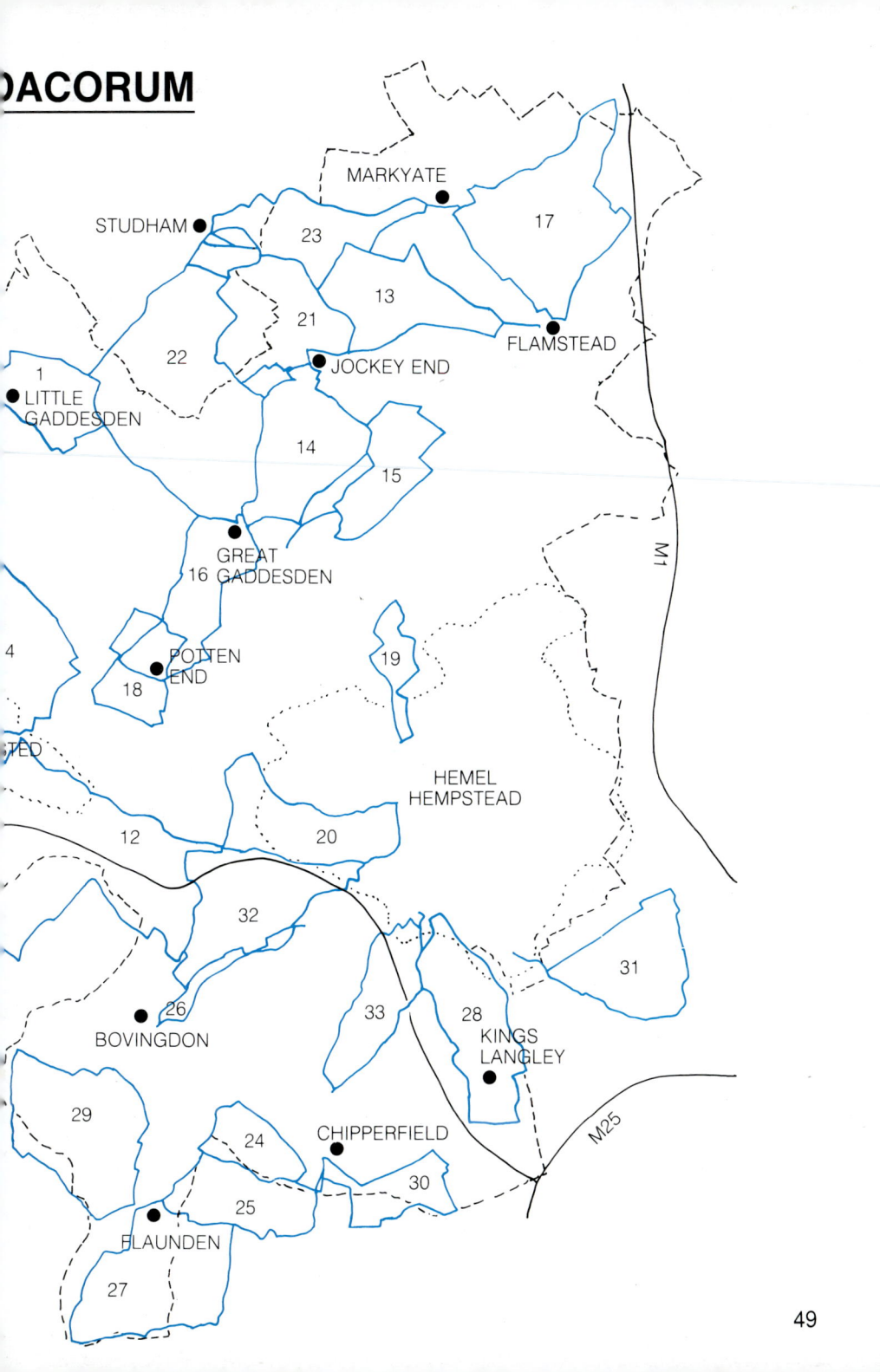

- STUDHAM
- MARKYATE
- 17
- 23
- 13
- 21
- FLAMSTEAD
- 22
- JOCKEY END
- 1
- LITTLE GADDESDEN
- 14
- 15
- GREAT
- 16 GADDESDEN
- M1
- 4
- POTTEN END
- 18
- 19
- HEMEL HEMPSTEAD
- 12
- 20
- 32
- 31
- 26
- 33
- 28
- BOVINGDON
- KINGS LANGLEY
- 29
- 24
- CHIPPERFIELD
- 25
- 30
- M25
- FLAUNDEN
- 27

49

WALK 20

LENGTH: 5½ MILES
TIME: 3 HOURS

- Ⓐ ST JOHNS CHURCH
- Ⓑ GRAND UNION CANAL
- Ⓒ WINKWELL
- Ⓓ WATER GARDENS

50

BOXMOOR - WINKWELL - HEMEL HEMPSTEAD

WALK 20

Park in lay-by (P) behind ST JOHNS CHURCH, BOXMOOR (A), near Dacorum Sports Centre (GR TL051 062). Buses pass nearby and Hemel Hempstead BR station is about ½ mile across Common.   **10.1**

1. Face downhill away from church and turn right along road over canal bridge. At end of bridge turn right down steps to towpath and GRAND UNION CANAL (B). With canal on RHS follow towpath past The Fishery Inn, then under bridge and past lock. Continue for one mile, under two more bridges, to swing bridge at WINKWELL (C).   **23.1**
   46

2. Cross bridge and pass Three Horseshoes PH. Take lane ahead under railway bridge and straight on up hill. Continue for ¾ mile, through Pouchen End, to top of hill. 300 yards after sharp bend to right, turn right over stile on LH bend.

3. Follow path, with hedge on LHS, through gateway into next field. Continue with small tree plantation on LHS to junction with hedged path. Turn right and follow this path to road.

4. Cross road and continue down path (SP Shrub Hill Common). Ignore paths to left and right and follow path down through trees. At end of field on LHS bear slightly left and then right to follow path into open grassland.

5. Follow alongside trees on LHS, past children's swings, then bear left uphill to footpath entrance next to houses. Follow path as it takes a dog-leg left up steps and then right to road. Cross to opposite road, Ashtree Way, and follow into Gravel Hill Terrace. As road continues into Woodland Avenue turn right into Woodland Close, then take footpath left down to road.

6. Across road and slightly to left, follow path up steps over road to path beside cemetery on RHS. Continue to road, then turn right and walk downhill with cemetery on RHS. Cross the road at the bottom (Heath Lane) and continue left into Cotterells Hill. Take the first turn left, Collett Road, then follow round to right into Astley Road. Continue to main road and cross over pedestrian crossing. Turn right and then left into Combe Street.

7. Cross Combe Street, and between car park entrance on RHS and River Gade on LHS, take path into WATER GARDENS (D). Follow through gardens, over a road, and along path to end of gardens. Cross road ahead, turn right and at traffic lights take footbridge over main road into Cotterells. Turn left, pass Kodak House, then keep right round Heath Park PH and Boxmoor Arts Centre. Cross road on left and return to car park past St John's Church.   **25.4**

WALK 21

LENGTH: 6 MILES
TIME: 3 HOURS

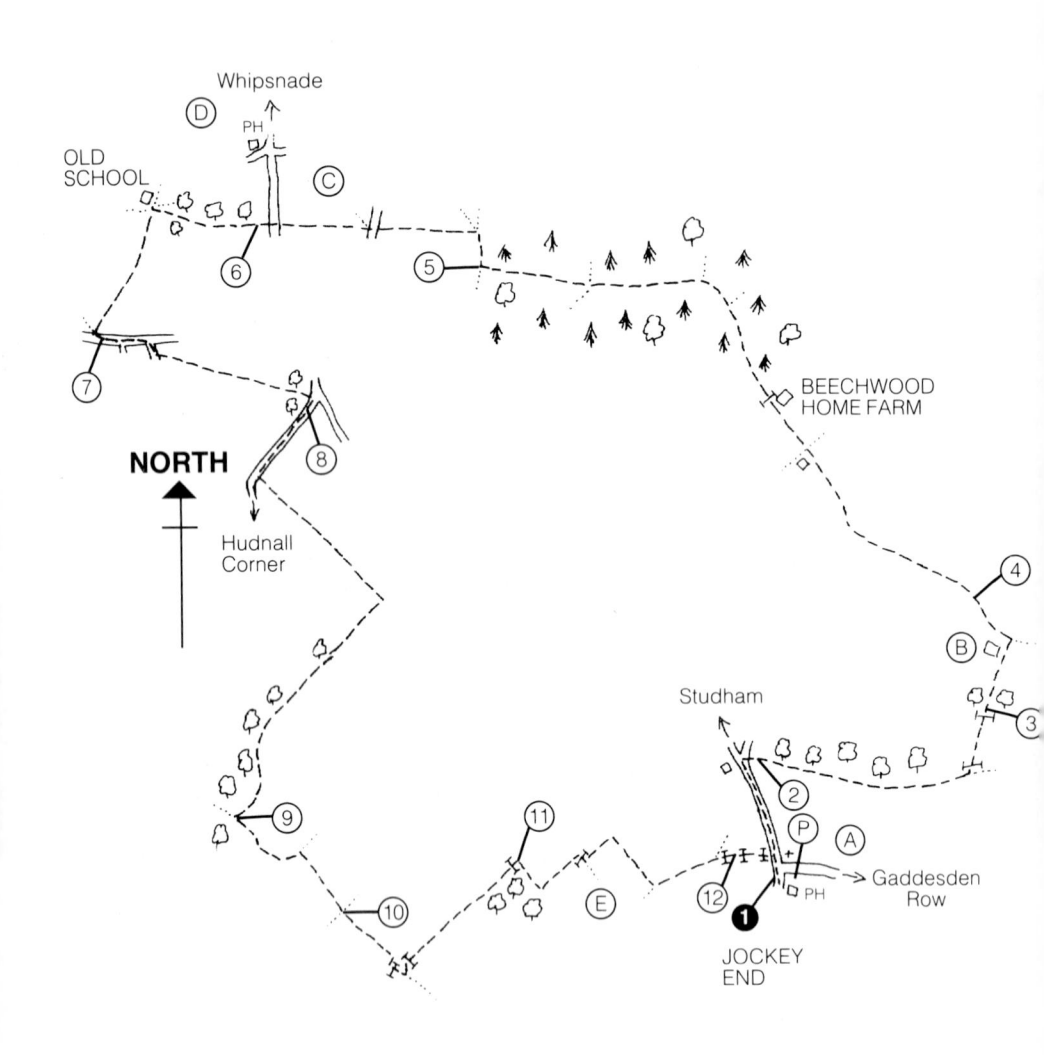

- Ⓐ **JOCKEY END**
- Ⓑ **BEECHWOOD HOUSE**
- Ⓒ **STUDHAM COMMON**
- Ⓓ **STUDHAM**
- Ⓔ **HEDGESWOOD COMMON**

JOCKEY END - STUDHAM   WALK 21

Park near THE PLOUGH (P) at JOCKEY END (A) (GR TL040 137). There is a limited bus service.   28

1. Walk along grass verge beside road to Studham for about 300 yards, to road on right on bend opposite farm ('Private Road' sign ahead).
2. Turn right along bridleway (SP). Follow this wide track, which can be muddy underfoot, with woods on LHS and hedge on RHS for about ½ mile. At field on left cross stile and bear right up hill to stile into wood.
3. Go straight ahead through wood, skirting to right of central group of trees, and emerge at the back of BEECHWOOD HOUSE (B), which is a school. Bear right and skirt the buildings, with boundary wall on LHS and playing fields on RHS. Turn left onto tarmac road and pass in front of school. Note view to right.   6
4. Continue on unsurfaced road for about ½ mile, passing 'Private Road' sign. At crossroads (Kennels Lodge) go straight on, pass Beechwood Home Farm on RHS and continue through gate/stile on wide track into Forestry Commission plantation. Keep to the track ahead for about ½ mile, ignoring turnings to left and right. Continue to gap into field.
5. Turn right along field edge with hedge on RHS. In corner path goes through some trees to emerge on corner of STUDHAM COMMON (C). Turn left and follow well-worn track, with hedge on LHS, to road. Cross road and continue on same line to next road. Down hill on right is STUDHAM village (D).   42.1
   42.2
6. Cross road and continue ahead on path with hedge on LHS. Path veers downhill to right through trees and emerges on grassy sward. Turn left towards Old School House, then take path which leads diagonally left uphill across open field. Go through gap onto road.
7. Turn left along road for about 200 yards and take last turning on right. Pass houses on LHS and take footpath diagonally left across open field (SP). Go through gap in hedge into playing field. Keep on to RH corner, with hedge on RHS. Follow path through trees onto road.
8. Turn right on road to LH bend, then turn left at SP into field. Follow field edge with hedge on LHS and at corner turn right. At first wood pass through hedge on LHS, turn right and follow path along RH edge of adjoining field.
9. Path eventually reaches junction with track. Turn left and follow this track through a gap into next field. Turn left along field edge, keeping hedge on LHS as it bends to left. Go through gap ahead and turn right (ignoring marker arrow). Follow field edge with hedge on RHS to track.
10. Cross over into next field and continue with hedge on LHS, turn right for a few yards then left over stile/gate. After a few yards turn left over stile and cross field towards LH edge of wood. Before reaching wood pass through wire fence on left and continue with fence, then wood, on RHS.
11. Over stile at corner of field turn right along edge of wood. At next corner turn left, then turn right at stile/gap in hedge onto HEDGESWOOD COMMON (E). Turn left to follow hedge on LHS, turning first right then left at field corners. Continue to corner of Common and cross stile between hedges to right of farm track.
12. Cross field with hedge on LHS to next stile, then continue along edge of next field to stile and over FB to road. Turn right on road to return to The Plough.

53

WALK 22

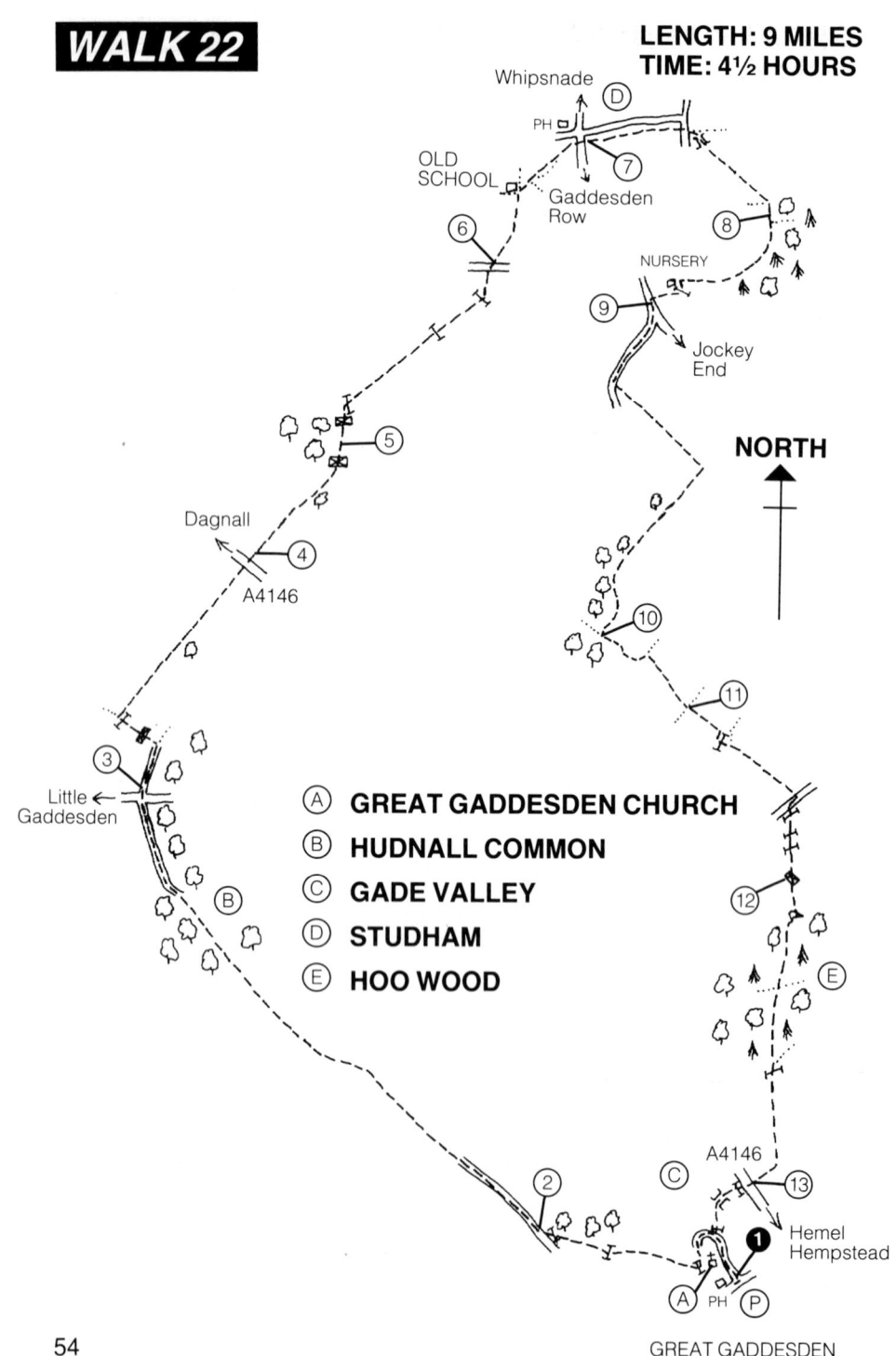

LENGTH: 9 MILES
TIME: 4½ HOURS

- Ⓐ **GREAT GADDESDEN CHURCH**
- Ⓑ **HUDNALL COMMON**
- Ⓒ **GADE VALLEY**
- Ⓓ **STUDHAM**
- Ⓔ **HOO WOOD**

54 GREAT GADDESDEN

GREAT GADDESDEN - HUDNALL COMMON - STUDHAM **WALK 22**

Park (P) in GREAT GADDESDEN, near The Cock and Bottle PH (GR TL029 112). The village has a limited bus service.

1. Walk along cul-de-sac with open ground on RHS and turning to CHURCH (A) on LHS. Pass school, then houses and follow road as it bends to left to reach row of garages. Cross forecourt to stile at left of garages. Over stile cross field diagonally right up hill to a gap in hedge. Continue on same line across next field to corner of woods. Cross stile and follow path with wood on RHS to stile onto road.   **22.1**
2. Turn right on road, which turns into a rough track and then later turns back to road. Continue for about 1¼ miles until HUDNALL COMMON (B) appears on RHS, then on for a further ¼ mile to crossroads.
3. Cross over main road onto private road. After about 200 yards turn left down a narrow hedged alleyway to a gate. Continue into field, keeping hedge on RHS to stile in far RH corner. Over stile turn right through gap in hedge. Follow path at edge of field with hedge on RHS and continue on same line downhill through next field to main road at bottom.
4. Take bridleway at SP opposite into field. Walk uphill with fence on LHS, through next field to disused gateway at edge of copse. Cross into field on left and continue uphill with hedge on RHS to metal gate. Note fine views of GADE VALLEY (C) and Ivinghoe Beacon from the top.   **22.2**
5. Pass through gate onto muddy track through wood for about 100 yards to next gate. Continue for about 40 yards to stile in hedge into field on right. Follow defined path diagonally left across field, over a stile and on same line across another field. Cross a second stile and walk along drive for 100 yards to road.
6. Cross road and take path at SP opposite diagonally right across a large field down to The Old School House. Bear right across grassy Common, taking either path through scrub to playing fields at STUDHAM crossroads (D).   **42**
7. Cross road signposted to Gaddesden Row and follow path along edge of Common with hedge on LHS, parallel to the Markyate road, for ¼ mile to road junction. Cross over onto concrete track and turn right, over FB, to take diagonal path uphill across Common to far corner. Follow path into next field, keeping to path at edge of field with trees on LHS.
8. Continue on path curving to right along field edge, ignoring paths into woodland. Go left through gap into another field and turn right to follow path round edge of field, with hedge on RHS. Pass nursery greenhouses and trees on RHS, and turn right at fence ahead to cross stile onto gravel drive. Turn right on drive out onto main road.
9. Turn left along road. Take right fork at junction and continue to LH bend. Turn left at SP through gap into field and along field edge with hedge on LHS. At corner turn right along field edge. At first wood pass through hedge on LHS and continue along edge of adjoining field with hedge on RHS.
10. Path eventually reaches junction with track. Turn left and follow track through gap into next field. Turn left along field edge and follow hedge on LHS as it bends to left. Go straight ahead through gap and turn right (ignoring marker arrow) along edge of next field to track.
11. Cross track and continue along LH edge of next field, turning right and after a few yards left over stile/gate. Take path ahead through scrub and then down track between fields and past farm to road. Turn right on road to bottom of slight dip and cross stile on left. Walk down field with hedge on LHS, cross next stile and continue with hedge now on RHS to another stile and then gateway on right.
12. Through gate turn left uphill to kissing gate into HOO WOOD (E). Bear right through wood along wide track, straight over path junction and on ignoring paths to left and right. Cross stile into open field and bear right across field to hedge. Follow this down to concrete drive past houses to main road.
13. Cross road to stile and cross meadow to footbridge over course of the River Gade. Follow path round to left and through gap in fence. Cross to stile into play area, turn left on road and return to Cock and Bottle PH.

55

WALK 23

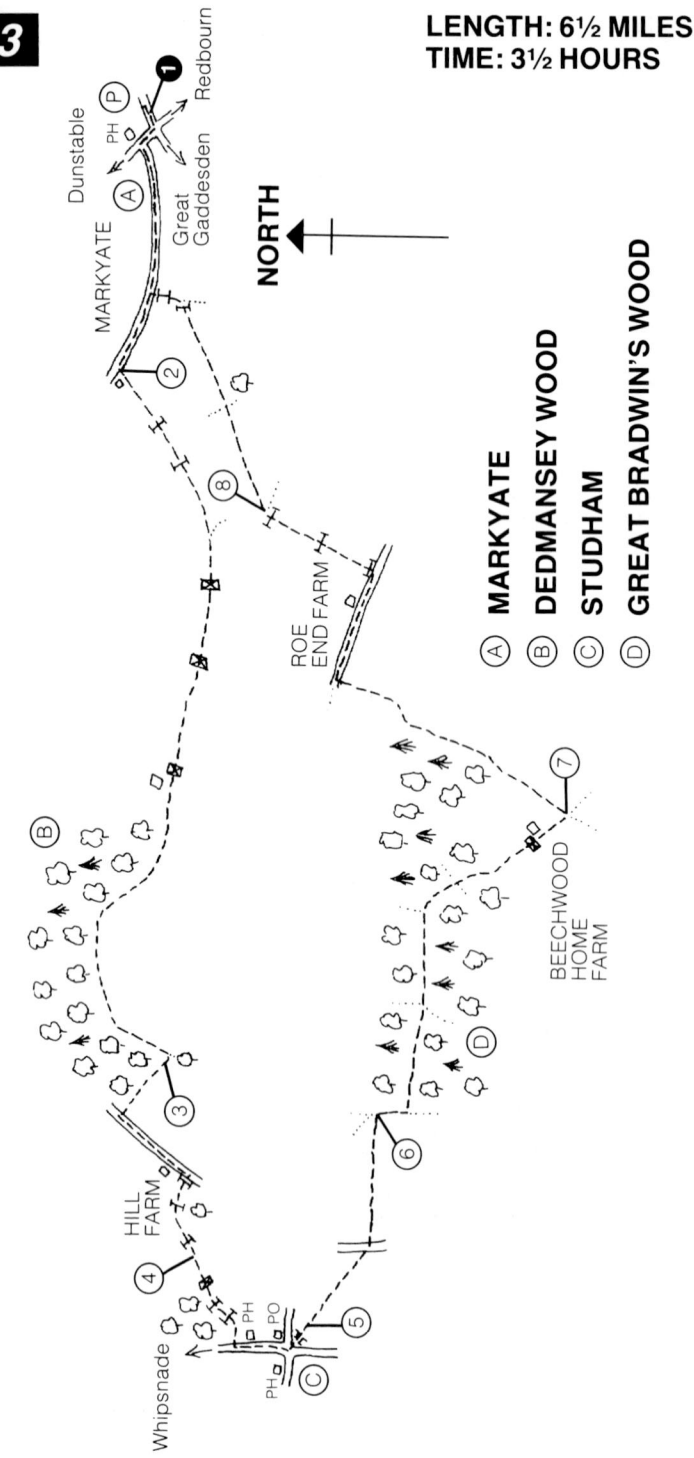

LENGTH: 6½ MILES
TIME: 3½ HOURS

- Ⓐ **MARKYATE**
- Ⓑ **DEDMANSEY WOOD**
- Ⓒ **STUDHAM**
- Ⓓ **GREAT BRADWIN'S WOOD**

MARKYATE - STUDHAM   *WALK 23*

Park in centre of MARKYATE (A) in Hicks Road Car Park (P) (GR TL062 163). **34**
There is a good bus service to Markyate.

1. Turn right from the car park and right again into main street, then take second road on left (Buckwood Road, SP to Studham). Walk along pavement till houses end, then continue along lane for about 250 yards. At house on left ('Gooseacre'), turn left on footpath at entrance to drive (SP Studham Common).

2. Follow narrow path between hedge on LHS and fence on RHS, over a stile and on along edge of field. Over next stile continue on path across open field, then turn right to follow track with hedge on LHS. Continue through three gateways. Pass old barns on RHS and at corner of wood follow path through gap in fence to left. Turn right and follow path along edge of DEDMANSEY WOOD (B) for over ½ mile.

3. At corner of field, with small copse ahead, turn sharp right on path through trees with wire fence on LHS. Continue beside wood to road. Turn left on road, pass Hill Farm on RHS and then about 100 yards further on turn right over stile. Bear slightly left across field, cross another stile, then follow a diagonal line left down to stile in far corner of field. Pass wood on LHS.

4. Over stile, follow path up field with hedge on RHS and at the top go through gate next to wood. Continue over one stile, then another into allotment field, then bear round to right and follow track to road. Cross the road and turn left past The Bell PH to STUDHAM crossroads (C).   **42**

5. At crossroads, cross FB on left over ditch onto open Common ahead. Take path diagonally uphill and cross road to join path running along top edge of Common with hedge on RHS.

6. At far corner of Common bear right through hedge into open field. Follow the path ahead for 100 yards, then turn left through hedge into GREAT BRADWIN'S WOOD (D). Follow track ahead through wood, going straight on at track junction. Ignore all paths to left and right and continue through gate/stile past Beechwood Home Farm on LHS.

7. A short distance past the farm turn left on track and continue for ½ mile to road. Turn right and follow road past entrance to Roe End Farm. After 150 yards turn left on path (SP Buckwood Road) and cross stile. With hedge on RHS, continue over next stile and keep on along RH field edge.

8. Over next stile take path ahead and bearing slightly to right across open field. Continue with hedge on RHS, over junction with track, to stile onto path behind houses. Turn left and follow path through wooden barrier, down to metal barrier at road. Turn right on road and return to Markyate.

WALK 24

LENGTH: 3 MILES
TIME: 1½ HOURS

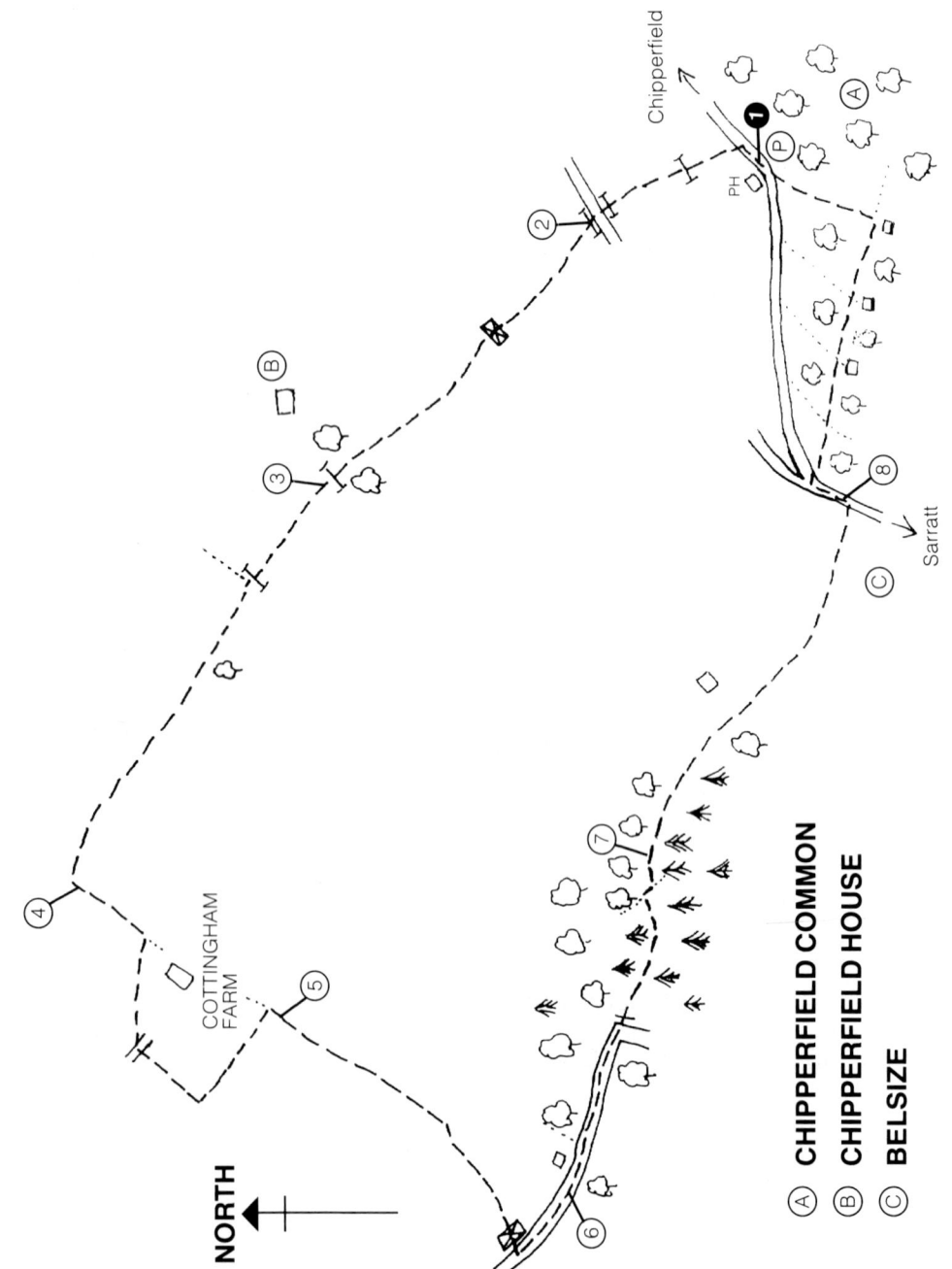

Ⓐ CHIPPERFIELD COMMON
Ⓑ CHIPPERFIELD HOUSE
Ⓒ BELSIZE

58

CHIPPERFIELD - BELSIZE   *WALK 24*

Park in car park (P) opposite The Windmill PH on CHIPPERFIELD COMMON (A) (GR TL040 014). Chipperfield villlage has a limited bus service.   **15.1**

1. Facing PH, turn right on lane towards village, then after a short distance turn left at SP. Walk along narrow path behind cottages to stile, then follow path diagonally right down to another stile in bottom corner of field.

2. Cross road and over stile opposite take path along RH edge of field. Continue through gate into next field and then through a wood to stile. CHIPPERFIELD HOUSE (B) may be visible through trees on RHS.   **15.3**

3. Keep hedge on RHS and continue over next stile. Take dog-leg right and then left into next field, and follow path ahead across open field. Go straight on with copse and then intermittent hedge on LHS.

4. Go through gap in hedge ahead and turn left along field edge. After about 100 yards take marked path diagonally right across field. Cross a concrete track and continue on path with hedge on RHS. Through gap in next hedge turn left and follow field edge, then through gap to farm track.

5. Turn right, with hedge on RHS. Follow track as it bends slightly right, leaving hedge on LHS. Go through gap beside wide gate and turn left on lane.

6. Follow lane past cottage on LHS into woods. At sharp RH bend go straight ahead over wooden barrier (SP Belsize). Take track through wood, which narrows and veers left downhill. Continue out of conifer plantation for about 30 yards, into more open woodland. Turn right at path junction, then just before re-entering plantation turn left uphill.

7. Follow path along plantation edge to top of hill, where woods on LHS give way to field. Continue to open field ahead and then straight on with hedge on LHS to road at BELSIZE (C).

8. Cross road and turn left on pavement. Turn right at junction up Windmill Hill, then immediately right onto bridleway (SP). Follow path over three path/track junctions, then at next track turn left. This track leads back to the Windmill PH and car park.

WALK 25

LENGTH: 5 MILES
TIME: 2½ HOURS

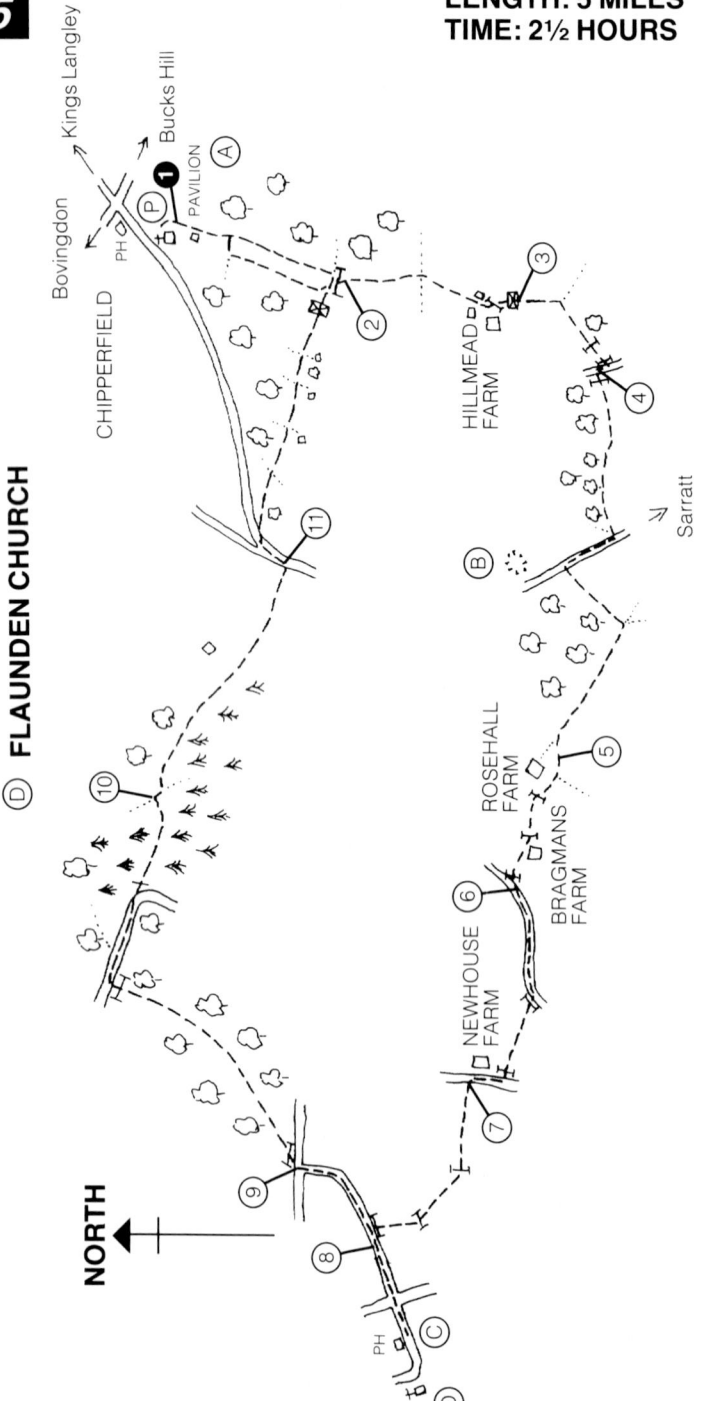

- Ⓐ CHIPPERFIELD COMMON
- Ⓑ ROSEHALL MOAT
- Ⓒ FLAUNDEN
- Ⓓ FLAUNDEN CHURCH

CHIPPERFIELD - FLAUNDEN   WALK 25

Park in car park (P) adjacent to Church on CHIPPERFIELD COMMON (A)   15.1
(GR TL043 015). Chipperfield village has a limited bus service.

1. Take path out of car park across front of cricket pavilion and then into woods with practice nets on LHS. Turn right at first path junction, then immediately left and on to major path junction at edge of wood. Go straight on over stile/metal gate.
2. Follow path with hedge on LHS to path junction at SP. Take private road ahead to Hillmeads Farm. Cross stile on left immediately after stable building, then turn right and follow waymarked track to next gate.
3. Continue on path with fence on LHS. When fence bends to left, follow waymarks to right along line of well-spaced trees to corner of small wood. Keep wood on LHS and continue to stile at bottom corner of field. Over stile go straight across next field to stile onto lane.
4. Turn right for about 40 yards to SP. Cross stile on left and follow waymarked path just within LH edge of wood. At road turn right. Further along this lane, in trees on RHS, is a MOAT (B). After 200 yards take first left along farm   41
track. Follow this track round wood on RHS to Rose Hall Farm.
5. Bear left round farm on concrete track but do not turn left. Cross stile and follow narrow path between hedges to another stile with building ahead. Over this turn right and then cross field diagonally left to stile in bottom LH corner.
6. Over stile turn left along lane for about ¼ mile. Take first marked path on right, at SP just before holly hedge. Over stile, cross field diagonally with farmhouse on RHS. Over next stile turn right down lane for about 100 yards, then left at next path.
7. Follow this well-defined path between hedge on RHS and fence on LHS to stile, then across an open field diagonally right. Over next stile follow hedge on LHS to stile onto road.
8. To visit FLAUNDEN (C), turn left along lane and go straight over crossroads   21
to Church (D) and Green Dragon PH. Return the same way, pass stile and   21.1
continue to T-junction.
9. Go straight on at T-junction on footpath (SP) over stile. Take path through wood to next stile into lane. Turn right on lane and at sharp RH bend go straight on over wooden barrier (SP Belsize). Follow track ahead which narrows and bears left down hill.
10. About 30 yards out of conifer plantation into more open woodland, turn right at path junction. Just before re-entering plantation, turn left uphill. Follow narrow path along plantation edge to top of hill, where woods on LHS give way to field. Continue on path to emerge into field, then with hedge on LHS follow down hill to road.
11. Cross road and turn left on pavement, then turn right up Windmill Hill. Turn right immediately onto bridleway (SP). Follow this path across driveways and on past houses on RHS to wooden gate. Continue to next path junction and turn left onto path which leads to a very old sweet chestnut tree in the middle of the path. Go straight on and follow path back to cricket field and car park.

WALK 26

LENGTH: 4 MILES
TIME: 2 HOURS

- Ⓐ **BURY WOOD**
- Ⓑ **ST LAWRENCES CHURCH**
- Ⓒ **BOVINGDON**

NORTH

62

FELDEN - BOVINGDON   **WALK 26**

Park at small parking area (P) on Felden Lane, overlooking Boxmoor Golf Course (GR TL040 052). This is about ½ mile from Hemel Hempstead BR station.

1. From the parking area walk past golf green to tree-lined footpath ahead and slightly to left. A few yards along this path turn left through kissing gate. Cross the RH corner of field to another kissing gate. Take path ahead over stile and along field edge to third kissing gate.

2. Turn right along road and at LH bend go straight on over stile. Follow well-defined path diagonally right across two fields and then along the edge of BURY WOOD (A). Ignore SP to right and continue to end of field. Cross stile and then another stile just ahead, then bear right to follow path round corner and along edge of field.

3. At far end of long field cross stile and follow path diagonally right across another field towards BOVINGDON CHURCH (B). Path continues over three more stiles and leads into lane. Turn left along lane into BOVINGDON (C). Note the old Well House at crossroads.   **9.2** **9.3**

4. Retrace steps down lane and bear left along yew-lined avenue to Church. Continue to road at far end of avenue, turn right and then left, following bridleway SP just visible from road. Follow this track past houses for one mile.

5. At the end of the houses, cross stile on left opposite Rainhill Spring. Follow path diagonally right across field and then between wooden fences. Continue straight on over private road, then down a very narrow alley to another road. Turn right to SP into wood on left.

6. Take left path at SP, which winds to left and up hill. Follow through wood, which is full of bluebells in spring, and then down well spaced log steps to unmade road. Cross to take path up hill opposite, with fence on RHS. At junction with bridleway turn right.

7. Continue on bridleway along top of golf course to private road, then on past kissing gates to return to car park area.

63

▼ FLAMSTEAD CHURCH (WALKS 13 & 17)

OLD TOWN, HEMEL HEMPSTEAD (WALK 19) ▲

▲ GREAT GADDESDEN (WALKS 14, 16 & 22)

▼ BOVINGDON (WALK 26)

▲ KINGS LANGLEY CHURCH (WALK 28)

WALK 27

LENGTH: 6 MILES
TIME: 3 HOURS

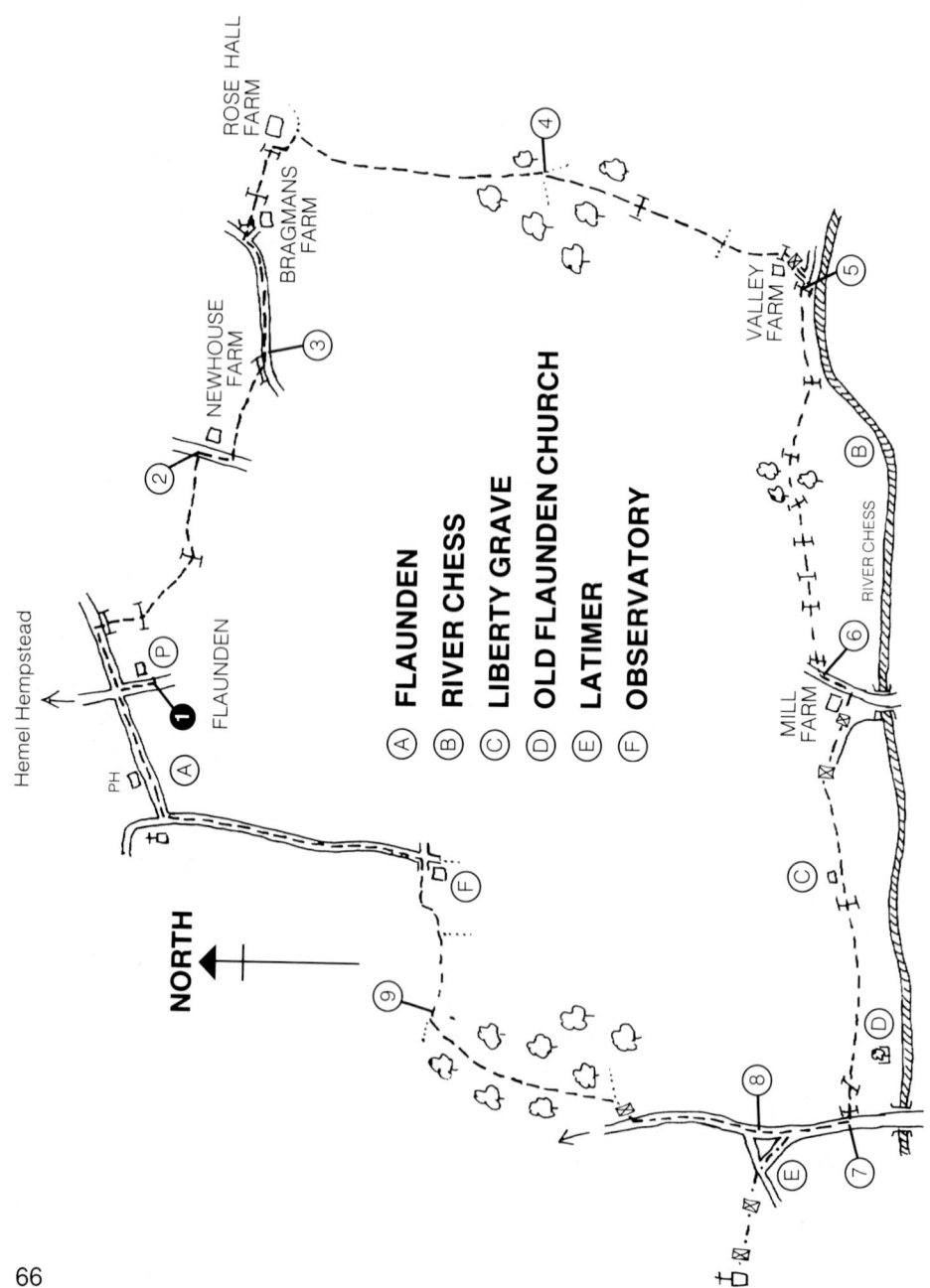

- Ⓐ FLAUNDEN
- Ⓑ RIVER CHESS
- Ⓒ LIBERTY GRAVE
- Ⓓ OLD FLAUNDEN CHURCH
- Ⓔ LATIMER
- Ⓕ OBSERVATORY

FLAUNDEN - CHESS VALLEY   *WALK 27*

Park in VILLAGE HALL CAR PARK (P) at FLAUNDEN (A) (GR TL017 007). **21**
No public transport is available.

1. From parking area turn right along road, then turn right again at crossroads. After 300 yards turn right over stile into field. Follow path ahead with hedge on RHS, over stile and diagonally left across field to next stile. Continue between hedge and fence to lane.

2. Turn right on lane, then left at footpath just past Newhouse Farm. Follow path along side of field with hedge on LHS, and when hedge bends to left bear right on path to stile. Cross stile and drop down to road.

3. Turn left on lane. After about ¼ mile, at SP on right beside entrance to Bragmans Farm, cross stile and then cross field diagonally to stile in far corner. Follow narrow path to stile and turn right on farm drive to skirt Rose Hall Farm on LHS. Turn right along first track, with fence on RHS, and continue into wood.

4. In wood take waymarked path ahead, which runs downhill to stile. Continue, crossing track near gateways, and eventually cross stile and go through gate into Valley Farm. Turn left on farm road and walk down to RIVER CHESS **14.4** (B).

5. The next sections of the walk follow the route of the Chess Valley Walk, with distinctive blue fish waymarks. Cross stile on right and with river on LHS follow path over next stile and on to stile into wood. Continue through wood, then on over three stiles, finally following fence on LHS to another stile onto lane.

6. Turn left on lane, then turn right on bridleway through farmyard (not FP to Flaunden). Pass through gate and follow river up to another gate. Keep to footpath ahead, passing the LIBERTY GRAVE (C) on RHS. Over stile **14.3** continue on waymarked path. When houses are seen ahead, keep straight on. NB : On left in this field is a fenced scrub area, which is the site of the OLD FLAUNDEN CHURCH (D), with spring rising nearby. Cross stile ahead **14.2** onto gravel track, then cross next stile at SP onto road.

7. Turn right on road into LATIMER (E). To visit church, take path between **14.1** houses at top of village green and continue uphill through two gates and across field. Return the same way.

8. At this point the route leaves the Chess Valley Walk. Follow road through village and continue to SP on right. (The road goes on to Flaunden, and in very wet weather may be easier than route described.) Turn right through gateway and follow bridleway up hill. Note views from the top. In the wood take left track and walk on for ½ mile to track junction.

9. Turn right on path out of wood and join a farm track. Keep left and follow track to junction opposite OBSERVATORY (F). Turn left along lane to Flaunden CHURCH and then turn right through village, passing The Green **21.1** Dragon PH on LHS. At crossroads turn right to return to Village Hall car park.

WALK 28

LENGTH: 5½ MILES
TIME: 3 HOURS

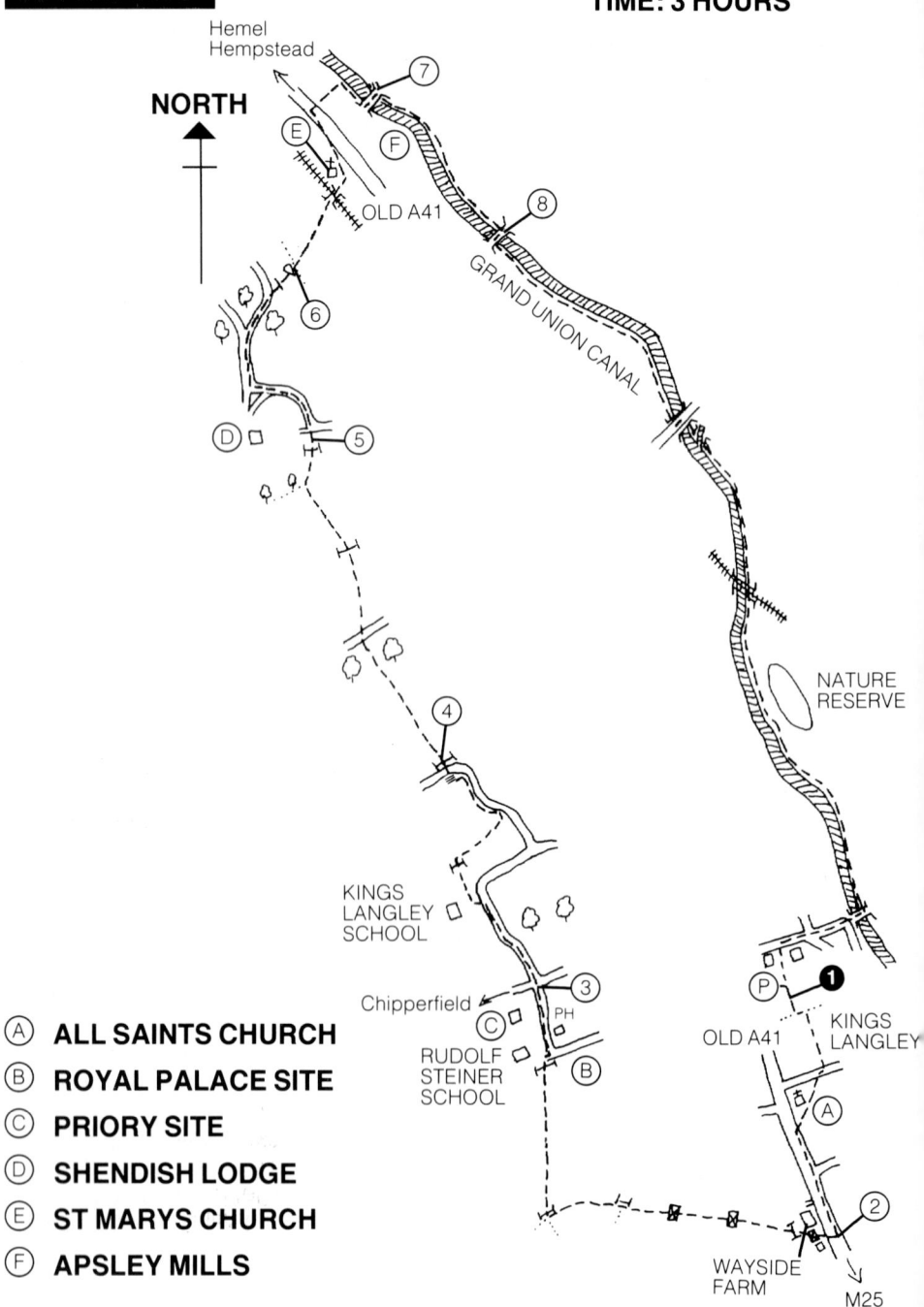

NORTH

Hemel Hempstead

OLD A41

GRAND UNION CANAL

NATURE RESERVE

KINGS LANGLEY SCHOOL

Chipperfield

RUDOLF STEINER SCHOOL

PH

OLD A41

KINGS LANGLEY

WAYSIDE FARM

M25

- Ⓐ **ALL SAINTS CHURCH**
- Ⓑ **ROYAL PALACE SITE**
- Ⓒ **PRIORY SITE**
- Ⓓ **SHENDISH LODGE**
- Ⓔ **ST MARYS CHURCH**
- Ⓕ **APSLEY MILLS**

KINGS LANGLEY - APSLEY *WALK 28*

Park in car park (P) at rear of Kings Langley library and Community Centre (GR TL073 028). The village is well served by buses and has a BR station.

1. From car park follow tarmac path into playing field, and turn left and then right past children's play area on LHS. Continue to road and turn right uphill, then cross over to take path diagonally through churchyard with ALL SAINTS CHURCH (A) on RHS. Turn left along main road and continue out of village to Wayside Farm on RHS. Cross road to take second turning into farmyard, with bungalow on LHS. **29.5**

2.* Go through gate and on over stile opposite. Follow track up hill along field edge and through two gates/stiles. Ignore first SP and continue uphill to next stile on right, with SP pointing towards school buildings. Cross this stile and take path across open field to another stile. Over this and keep on to road, passing former ROYAL PALACE site (B) on RHS. Turn right, away from Rudolf Steiner School, then left along road. **29.3**

3. On LHS just before crossroads is the site of the OLD PRIORY (C). Go straight on at crossroads along Love Lane, with Kings Langley Common on RHS. After about ¼ mile turn left into school entrance, then right on footpath just before school gates. Follow this path as it skirts school grounds, crossing one stile. Ignore first metal steps to road and continue along school perimeter fence. At next steps on RHS cross road to stile opposite. **29.2**

4. With hedge on LHS, follow path along field edge and descend slightly to stile. Continue down steep bank through woodland to lane. Cross over and follow track opposite up to stile, then take path across field. At edge of trees bear right to skirt grounds of SHENDISH LODGE (D) on LHS. **2.4**

5. Over next stile, then cross access drive and grass bank to lane. Bear left along lane, fork right to crossroads and then turn right. Enter wood and at the next junction bear right. Continue for a short distance until lane bends left. Go straight on, passing an iron barrier and going through swing gate onto golf course.

6. Follow path on line of SP downhill across golf course, keeping to band of trees. At bottom of hill cross railway footbridge into churchyard. Bear left past ST MARY'S CHURCH (E) to road. Turn left on pavement to Kent's Avenue, then cross road to take footpath between fences. **2.2**

7. Path leads to canal bridge. Over canal turn left down steps onto towpath, then left again under bridge. Follow towpath with canal on RHS through industrial area (F), past lock to bridge No 154. Go over bridge and continue on towpath towards Nash Mills Lock. At next lock follow path up onto Red Lion Lane.

8. Cross canal and take ramp on right then cross footbridge over River Gade. Continue along towpath with canal on RHS. Canal passes under railway bridge and presently passes a nature reserve on LHS before reaching Kings Langley. Cross footbridge near houses and go straight on through car park to road. Turn up hill and return to car park.

WALK 29

LENGTH: 5½ MILES
TIME: 3 HOURS

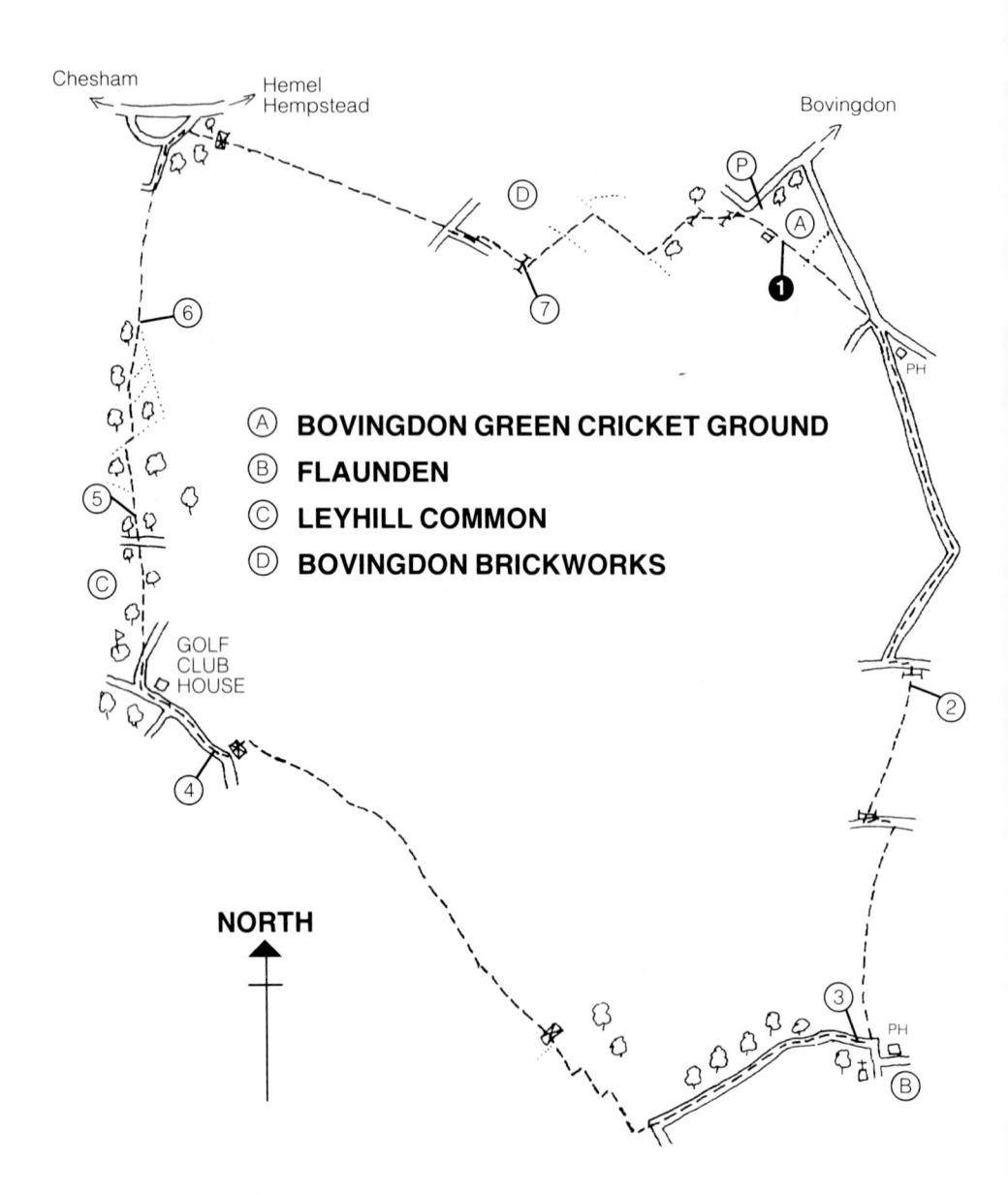

- Ⓐ BOVINGDON GREEN CRICKET GROUND
- Ⓑ FLAUNDEN
- Ⓒ LEYHILL COMMON
- Ⓓ BOVINGDON BRICKWORKS

NORTH

BOVINGDON GREEN - FLAUNDEN - LEY HILL COMMON

WALK 29

Park beside BOVINGDON GREEN (A), just south of Bovingdon village. Some space (P) is often available near the cricket pavilion (GR TL010 029). There is a regular weekday bus service.   **9**

1. Cross the Green, passing cricket field, towards Royal Oak PH. With PH on LHS, walk down Middle Lane for ¾ mile to T- junction. Turn left and after 50 yards turn right over stile at SP.

2. Follow path between fence and hedge to road, cross stile and turn left. At SP 100 yards ahead turn right on path to FLAUNDEN (B). The Church (St Mary Magdalene) can be seen ahead through trees and on reaching the village The Green Dragon PH is on LHS.   **21**

3. Turn right on road and walk downhill to Flaunden Bottom. When road bears left follow FP/bridleway up the track ahead. Near the top of the hill, after a series of bends, leave main track and go straight on through gate to follow grassy track along field edge, between fence and hedge. Path opens out on right and eventually meets lane at gateway.

4. Turn right along lane and then right again into lane just past Golf Clubhouse. 100 yards ahead turn left at SP onto golf course at LEY HILL COMMON (C). Fork right behind a bunker, with green on LHS, to enter trees. Follow path through trees and across two fairways to road.   **30**

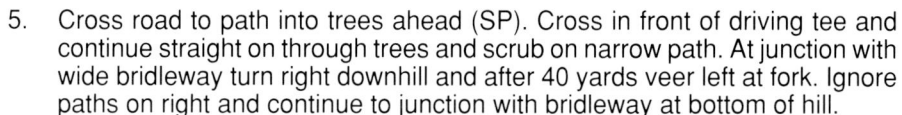

5. Cross road to path into trees ahead (SP). Cross in front of driving tee and continue straight on through trees and scrub on narrow path. At junction with wide bridleway turn right downhill and after 40 yards veer left at fork. Ignore paths on right and continue to junction with bridleway at bottom of hill.

6. Turn left to join bridleway along edge of field and continue for ¼ mile to lane. Turn right, then right again at lane junction. After 50 yards turn right again on bridleway (SP) into trees. Go through gate and follow bridleway for ½ mile to road junction at Pudds Cross. Take road opposite, then after 50 yards take footpath on left (SP) along fence skirting BOVINGDON BRICKWORKS (D).   **9.1**

7. Cross stile and turn left through brickworks, across first track to second track junction. Turn right, then after 200 yards turn left down narrow path through trees, behind gardens. Cross stile at far end and take path through paddock to further stile. Turn left on driveway, then bear right through hedge on to Bovingdon Green and return to cricket pavilion.

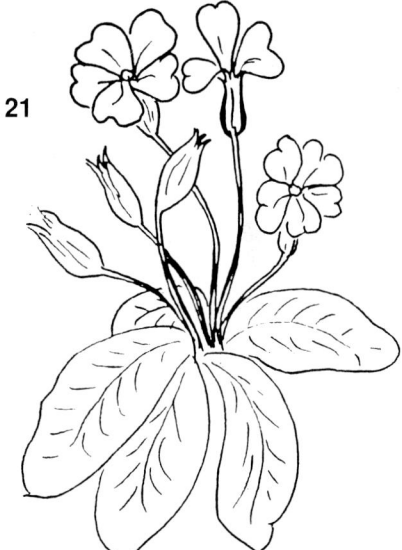

71

WALK 30

LENGTH: 4 MILES
TIME: 2 HOURS

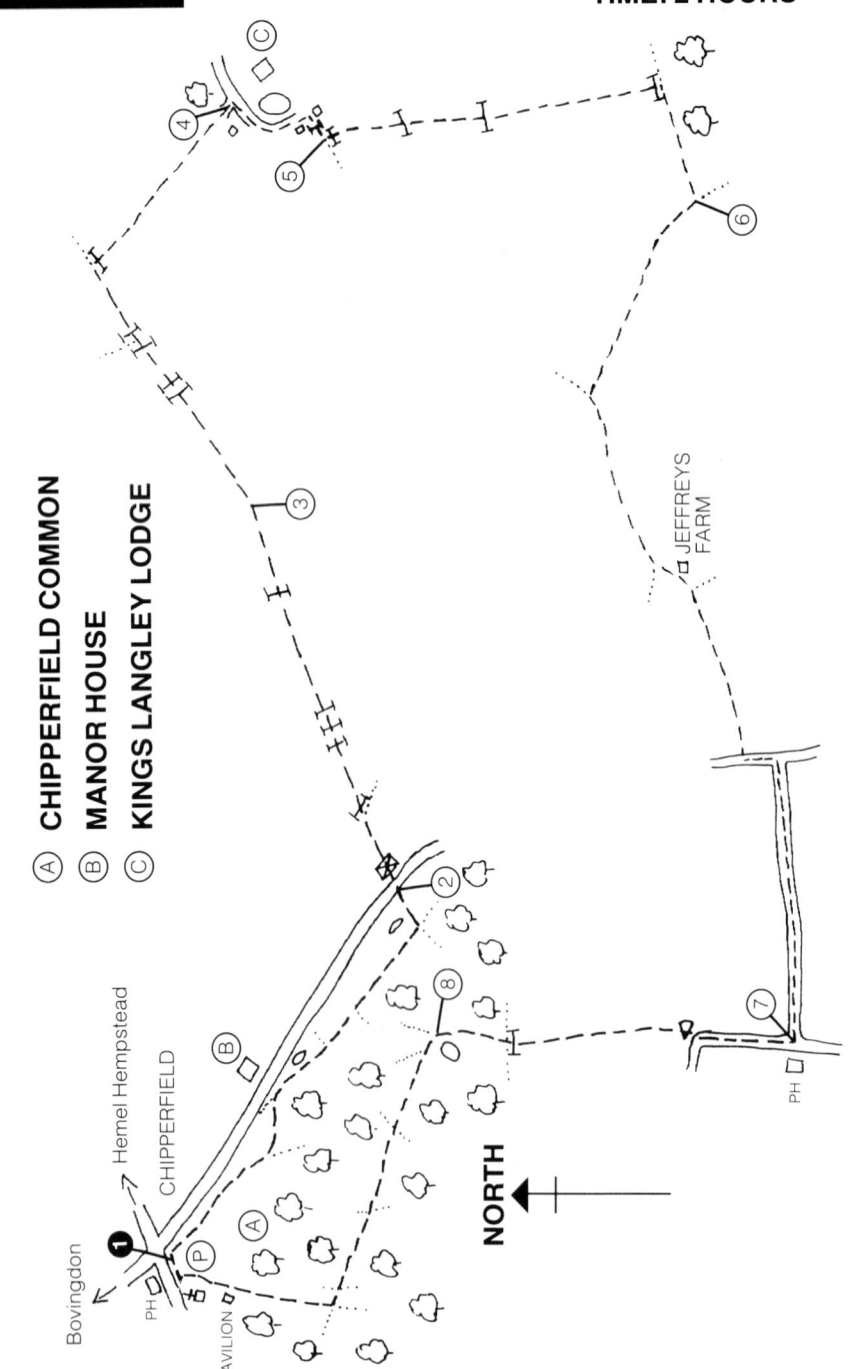

- Ⓐ **CHIPPERFIELD COMMON**
- Ⓑ **MANOR HOUSE**
- Ⓒ **KINGS LANGLEY LODGE**

72

CHIPPERFIELD COMMON - LANGLEY LODGE

WALK 30

Park in car park (P) adjacent to Church on CHIPPERFIELD COMMON (A) (GR TL043 015). Chipperfield village has a limited bus service.

15.1

1. Facing away from Two Brewers PH, bear left around cricket field with road on LHS. At SP take clear path into woods. At first marker post bear left on smaller path. Follow almost to road (Note MANOR HOUSE (B) ahead) and turn right along bridleway, passing pond on LHS. Ignore paths on left and right, then just past small pond turn left on path to road.

15.6

15.4

2. Cross road to private drive with gate/stile (SP Kings Langley). Go along drive, cross first stile on left and cross field to three further stiles into large field with hedge on LHS. Follow path along field edge to next stile, then continue on same line into valley.

3. At bottom corner of field go straight on along narrow path through bushes and continue uphill between fences. Cross two stiles near top of hill and then continue with fences either side over two more stiles. Further on turn right over stile at SP and take path which leads through farm buildings to T-junction in lane.

4. Turn right and follow lane round LH bend into farmyard. Note KINGS LANGLEY LODGE (C) beyond lake on LHS. Turn right between house and farm buildings and take footpath (SP) over stile. Continue between fences to another stile 100 yards ahead on left.

29.1

5. Cross stile and then another one across field. Follow path diagonally right to far RH corner of next field. Over stile keep to field edge with fence on RHS and continue towards wood. Cross stile and turn right to follow path along edge of wood, eventually descending to track.

6. Turn right on track. Near top of hill bear left and continue on track, which becomes tarmac road. Pass farm on LHS and carry on to T-junction. Turn left and shortly afterwards turn right into Quickmoor Lane. Follow lane for ¼ mile to T-junction at Cart and Horses PH.

7. Turn right along lane towards Penmans Green. When lane bends left, continue straight on (SP Kings Langley). Go through kissing gate and take path between fences. Cross stile into woodland and take path straight ahead round pond on LHS.

8. Fork left and continue through wood, ignoring paths to left and right, for about ¼ mile. At major path junction turn right along path leading to open space. Emerge from trees onto cricket field, and cross in front of pavilion to return to car park.

WALK 31

LENGTH: 5½ MILES
TIME: 3 HOURS

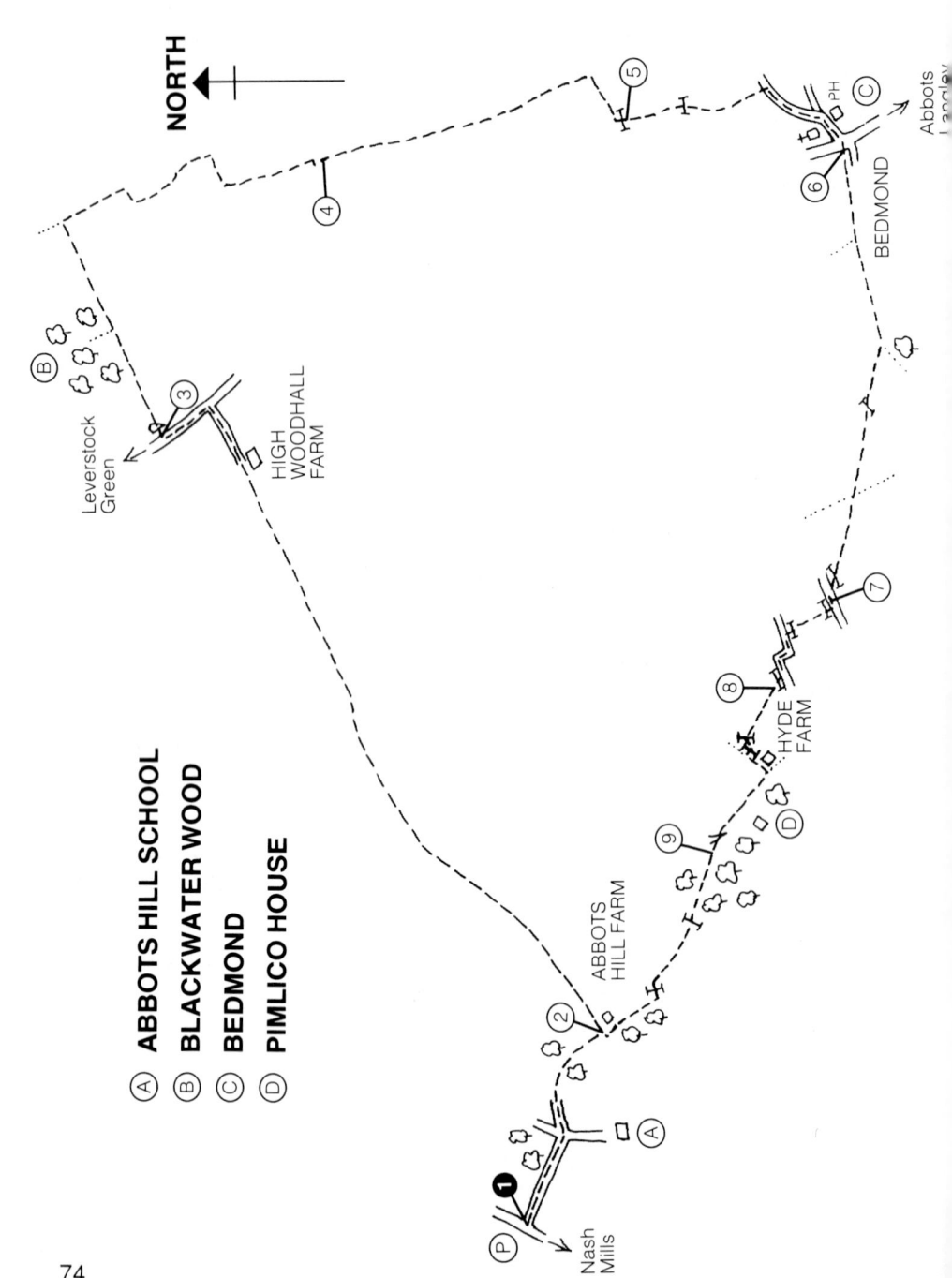

NORTH

Ⓐ ABBOTS HILL SCHOOL
Ⓑ BLACKWATER WOOD
Ⓒ BEDMOND
Ⓓ PIMLICO HOUSE

74

NASH MILLS - BEDMOND **WALK 31**

Park on roadside at bottom of BUNKERS LANE (P), near junction with Highwoodhall Lane (GR TL073 047). Buses run along Belswains Lane, and Apsley BR station is about one mile away.

1. Turn up Highwoodhall Lane. On LHS note Long Deans Nature Reserve, mixed woods and grassland owned by the Herts & Middlesex Wildlife Trust. Follow the lane to crossroads of driveways at entrance to ABBOTS HILL SCHOOL (A), and bear left uphill towards Abbots Hill Farm. **2.1**
2. At entrance to farm turn left onto bridleway with hedge on RHS (very muddy at times). Follow bridleway for about one mile to join lane at Highwoodhall Farm, and continue on lane past sports field to road. Cross road and turn left.
3. 100 yards ahead on right go through kissing gate into large field. Follow path along field edge past BLACKWATER WOOD (B) to T-junction with track. **5.1** Turn right on track with hedge on RHS and continue through bends and on past end of hedge. Turn right on path which veers right then left to rejoin hedge on LHS. Continue to corner of field, turn right for a few yards and then left through gap in hedge next to telegraph pole.
4. Take path across field following line of trees. Pass through hedge into next field and continue on same line to far side. Turn right with hedge on LHS. In corner of field cross stile to left into another field.
5. Follow path across field, with hedge/fence on RHS, to stile in far RH corner of field. Cross stile and take path which passes through gap in hedge on right and continues between hedge and fence to lane. Turn right past White Hart PH to BEDMOND (C) crossroads. Note Church of the Ascension on RHS. **5.4** A village shop is nearby on LHS.
6. At crossroads take path opposite (SP Hemel Hempstead & Kings Langley). Follow path past houses and straight on across field to edge of wood. At footpath marker cross field on path diagonally right to stile. Continue on same line to cattle trough in centre of large field, then straight on to stile into lane. (Ignore paths to left and right.)
7. Turn left up lane and almost immediately right over stile. Take path along field edge with hedge on RHS. Cross stile into lane and turn left, round bend to right and then at LH bend cross stile on right.
8. Cross field diagonally left to far corner by farm buildings. Cross stile and immediately right over second stile. Turn left down track through farm. At path junction turn right down edge of field with trees on LHS. Halfway down field pass through an old kissing gate on left.
9. Continue to right downhill through woodland to stile. Over stile take path bearing left uphill across corner of field. Note view of PIMLICO HOUSE (D) **5.3** behind. With hedge on LHS continue up to next corner of field and cross stile. Follow path to right through trees to join track at Abbots Hill Farm. Turn left downhill and straight over crossroads back to Bunkers Lane.

75

WALK 32

LENGTH: 6 MILES
TIME: 3 HOURS

Ⓐ **ST JOHNS CHURCH**
Ⓑ **BURY WOOD**
Ⓒ **LITTLE HAY GOLF CLUBHOUSE**
Ⓓ **WINKWELL**

76

BOXMOOR - LITTLE HAY - WINKWELL

WALK 32

Park in lay-by (P) behind ST JOHN'S CHURCH, BOXMOOR (A), near Dacorum Sports Centre (GR TL051 062). Buses stop nearby. From Hemel Hempstead BR station turn right along main road, then right up Roughdown Road and join walk at Section 2. **10.1**

1. Face downhill away from church and turn right along main road over canal. Turn right down steps onto towpath, then under bridge and right through kissing gate. Bear right across field to FB over River Bulbourne, then follow path to gate. Cross main road and walk up terraced street opposite (Russell Place). Turn right along Catlin Street, then left onto Roughdown Road.

2.* Cross railway bridge, then take track ahead which bears right along the bottom of Roughdown Common. Cross footbridge over A41 bypass, and follow path downhill with bypass on RHS for a short distance before turning left into trees. Ignore path which crosses at right angles but bear left at next fork. At next track junction turn right and continue to road.

3. Turn left uphill on road. After about 150 yards take private road on right across golf course towards Felden Lodge. Just before gatehouse turn right along bridleway through belt of trees along top of golf course. Where bridleway bears away to right, continue ahead on footpath and follow as it bears right downhill to unsurfaced lane.

4. Turn left up lane. Continue as track narrows to path, and just before reaching edge of wood turn right up bank. Follow clear path through BURY WOOD (B), within sight of field on LHS. Just before reaching houses turn right on path down to road.

5. Turn right on road, then after about 50 yards left at SP up very narrow alley. At the top cross private road and keep on between fences to field. Cross field diagonally left to SP and stile into lane, then turn right along lane for about $^1/_2$ mile. Where the lane turns right, continue straight ahead on a track that narrows as it passes the last house on LHS. About 200 yards further on, turn right between two gates down a narrow path (SP). Follow through bends to right and left to main road.

6. Turn right and walk along grass verge. About 150 yards beyond entrance to Little Hay Golf Complex cross road to driveway beside Little Hay Cottage. Cross stile at SP on right and take path ahead through trees, bearing round to meet road on left. Turn right and follow road to GOLF CLUB HOUSE (C). Continue as road bears left and when road ends near buildings turn right along path at SP. Follow round top edge of golf course to SP pointing downhill. **32**

7.* Turn left and follow path down across golf course past another SP. At next SP bear left, then turn right to take path over bridge across A41 bypass. Follow hedge on LHS down to gate/stile. Over stile follow grassy track to main road. There is a Little Chef cafe a short distance to the left.

8. Cross road and turn right on pavement, then take first turning on left, WINKWELL (D). At canal bridge, with The Three Horseshoes PH opposite, turn right along towpath. Follow towpath for about 1$^1/_2$ miles back to Boxmoor. On the way pass a lock and go under a railway bridge, then pass another two locks and go under another two bridges (to the LHS of second bridge is The Fishery PH). At next bridge climb steps to road and turn left to return to car park. **46**

77

WALK 33

LENGTH: 5 MILES or 6 MILES
TIME: 2½ HOURS or 3 HOURS

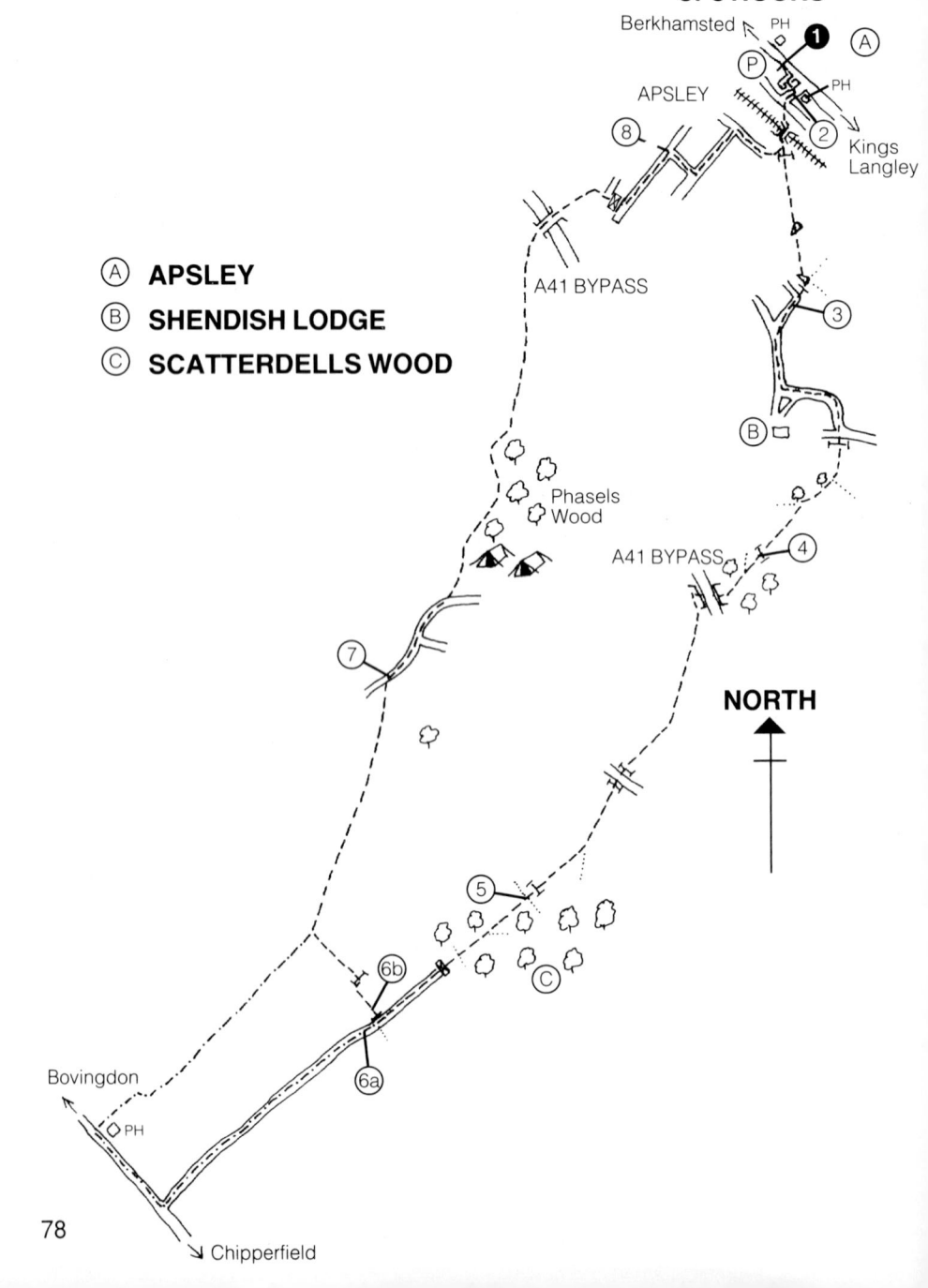

- Ⓐ **APSLEY**
- Ⓑ **SHENDISH LODGE**
- Ⓒ **SCATTERDELLS WOOD**

Berkhamsted
APSLEY
Kings Langley
A41 BYPASS
Phasels Wood
A41 BYPASS
NORTH
Bovingdon
Chipperfield

78

APSLEY - SCATTERDELLS WOOD   WALK 33

Park in the car park (P) in London Road, APSLEY (A), just opposite the Post   2
Office (GR TL057 054). There are regular weekday buses. From Apsley BR
station turn left onto London Road, and after less than half a mile turn left to join
walk at Weymouth Street (Section 2).

1. From car park turn right on pavement beside London Road and then right at first turning (Avia Close). Turn left along path through children's play area, then right at the end along Weymouth Street.

2. At T-junction cross the road and bear left on footpath between houses (SP Shendish and Chipperfield). Cross railway bridge, then cross stile into field. Take path diagonally left up the field and pass through swing gate. Shortly afterwards, at path junction with SP, turn right through swing gate and then past metal barrier to lane.

3. Go straight ahead on lane and at T-junction turn left. Just beyond Paddock Cottage, turn left beside a sports field. The lane bears right, then as it bears left go straight on up grassy bank and cross access drive to SHENDISH (B). Take **2.4** path ahead over a stile and then on around the perimeter of Shendish grounds. Ignore first path on left, then about 150 yards after entering field bear left across field to stile.

4.* Continue on path into wood, then as path joins track follow downhill to lane. Turn right onto Rucklers Lane and walk under A41 bypass. Turn immediately sharp left and follow path uphill to top of hedge. Bear right across field to stile onto lane. Cross lane and stile opposite, then follow path across field. Part way across bear right on path downhill to stile. Cross stile into SCATTERDELLS WOOD (C).

5. Take path ahead, straight across track at junction, then down and up hill opposite through woodland. As the path levels out and joins a track from the left, continue straight ahead. Go straight over next track junction to gate/stile onto lane. Follow lane ahead for about 300 yards.

6a. LONGER ROUTE : To visit CHIPPERFIELD, continue along lane for about ½   **15** mile to T-junction. Chipperfield village is about ½ mile along road to left. On return, continue past The Boot PH and turn right at SP along wide track past houses. Follow track along edge of very large field, and at SP on corner bear left diagonally on path to lane.

6b. SHORTER ROUTE : Just before SP on left, take path to right through metal barrier and between hedges. Dogleg right and then left over stile, then follow field edge with hedge on LHS. At SP on corner, take path diagonally right across large open field.

7.* Turn right on lane, pass turning on right (Barnes Lane), and at RH bend turn left at SP. Follow this bridleway for one mile, passing Phasels Wood Scout Complex on RHS. When track reaches A41 bypass, go straight on over bridge and then on along track with hedge on RHS. Follow track as it bends right to gate, then through gate turn left downhill on road.

8. Halfway down hill turn right into St George's Road and continue on path down to West Valley Road. Turn left, and at bottom of road turn right along King Edward Street. Carry on up hill to end of road, then left on footpath to railway footbridge. Cross railway and retrace steps to car park.

PLACES OF INTEREST

1. ALDBURY

1.1 VILLAGE
This is one of the prettiest villages in Hertfordshire, complete with pond, green, stocks and whipping post. The manor house is 300 years old.

1.2 ST JOHNS CHURCH
The church is mostly 14th century and contains monuments to the knights and ladies of the three main local houses : the Manor, Pendley and Stocks.

1.3 PUBLIC HOUSES
The Greyhound and The Valiant Trooper

1.4 ALDBURY NOWERS
Aldbury Nowers consists of two areas of woodland and a chalk grassland area managed as a nature reserve by the Herts & Middlesex Wildlife Trust. Strawberry Woods was badly damaged in the 1990 gales : part has been replanted, while some areas have been left to regenerate naturally. Turlhangar Wood is an ancient beechwood which has also suffered gale damage. Duchies Piece is an important relic of herb-rich chalk grassland, with characteristic flowers and grasses providing habitat for a wide variety of butterflies.
Pitstone Hill, above Aldbury Nowers, has evidence of neolithic flint mines and later prehistoric ramparts. There are fine views, including Pitstone Windmill.

2. APSLEY

2.1 ABBOTS HILL
John Dickinson built this house for himself overlooking his Nash Mills property in 1836. He later added an observatory. The front door, above which the letter 'D' is carved in stone, was the only door in the original house : the owner liked to keep an eye on all comings and goings. The building is now a private school.

2.2 ST MARYS CHURCH
The church was designed by Joseph Clarke, but Charles Longman was mostly responsible for its construction in 1871.

2.3 MILLS
John Dickinson bought Apsley Mill in 1809. He installed paper making machinery and later in 1815 introduced steam power. The mill became one of six in the area.

2.4 SHENDISH LODGE
Originally known as the Manor of Langley, occupation on this site can be traced back to 1086. The present building was built in the 1850s for Charles Longman, John Dickinson's partner. It is now a private conference and leisure centre.

2.5 PUBLIC HOUSES
Several, including The Oddfellows Arms, The Red Lion and The White Lion.

3. ASHLEY GREEN

3.1 ST JOHNS CHURCH
The parish of St John the Evangelist was created in 1875 and the church was consecrated in the same year. It is built in 13th century style, with flint and stone dressings.

3.2 PUBLIC HOUSE
The Golden Eagle.

4. ASHRIDGE

4.1 BRIDGEWATER MONUMENT
A Doric column 108' high, erected in 1832 for the 3rd Duke of Bridgewater to commemorate his pioneering work on the English canal network. Open Easter - October, Monday-Thursday 2-5 pm, weekends 2-5.30 pm. (Charge for admission.)

4.2 ESTATE
The estate is owned by the National Trust, and extends along the Chiltern ridge from Berkhamsted to Ivinghoe Beacon. There is a shop and information centre near the Monument (same opening hours) with a tea kiosk open on summer weekends only. The building a short distance north of Monument Green is a reconstuction of an earlier tea house, and is now used as a base for volunteer conservation teams.

4.3 MANAGEMENT COLLEGE
This site was first occupied by a monastery founded in 1283, of which little apart from the crypt survives. After the Dissolution in 1537 it became a royal residence, then a private mansion. The present building is one of the most extensive and picturesque Neo Gothic mansions in the country, begun in 1808 by James Wyatt and completed by his nephew, Jeffrey Wyattville. Early landscaping of the original 4000 acre Park was carried out by Capability Brown (ca 1760). Humphry Repton devised the first designs for the gardens (ca 1814). The gardens (but not the college) are open to the public at weekends from Easter - October 2-6 pm. (Charge for admission.)

5. BEDMOND

5.1 BLACKWATER WOOD
Blackwater Wood is a part of the Crown's Gorhambury Estate and is open to the public by permission. The path along the edge of the wood is a newly-designated right of way.

5.2 CHURCH OF THE ASCENSION
This iron church was originally built in 1880.

5.3 PIMLICO HOUSE
This is a brick-by-brick copy of Chipperfield Manor and was built in 1921. It is a long narrow house, only the width of one room, and was once occupied by the late Lord Arran. The grounds cover nearly 60 acres.

5.4 VILLAGE
This was the birthplace of Nicholas Breakspear, the only English Pope. Born a poor farmer's son, he became a monk at St Albans Abbey and was elected to the Papal Throne in 1154 as Adrian IV.

5.5 PUBLIC HOUSES
The Bell Inn and The White Hart

6. BEECHWOOD HOUSE

A nunnery was founded on this site in the 13th century. After the Dissolution in 1537 a house was built by Captain Page, some of which may still be incorporated in the H-shaped south front with high chimneys. In 1702 Sir Edward Sebright came from Worcestershire, married the heiress of the local Saunders family and built the magnificent north-east front, facing grounds originally laid out by Capability Brown. Since 1964 the buildings have been occupied by a private school.

7. BERKHAMSTED

7.1 CASTLE
The first castle was built by Robert of Mortain, half-brother of William the Conqueror. It had many subsequent owners including Edward, the Black Prince, but eventually fell into disrepair in the 15th century. Much of the stone was used in other buildings in the town. It is now in the care of English Heritage and is open Monday-Saturday and after 2pm on Sundays. Admission free.

7.2 COMMON
Berkhamsted Common was originally part of the Ashridge Estate. In 1866 the then owner, the second Lord Brownlow, attempted to enclose it. Legal proceedings were taken against Mr Augustus Smith, a local dignitary and MP for Truro, who took a counter action for the right of common pasture. Lord Brownlow died before the case could be heard, but the right of common pasture was won and still exists today. When Lord Brownlow's successor Adelbert died in 1921 the Ashridge Estate was sold to pay death duties. Part of Berkhamsted Common was acquired for a Golf Club, the remainder was bought by public subscription for the National Trust. It is now one of the largest commons in the country.

7.3 ALPINE MEADOW
This is a small chalk grassland reserve managed by the Herts & Middlesex Wildlife Trust to preserve wildflowers and butterflies.

7.4 TOWN
It was at Berkhamsted that William the Conqueror was received as King. The town lies on an important line of communications, with the Canal, the old A41 and the railway. There are numerous interesting buildings, including Berkhamsted School, the Court House and Dean Incent's House.

7.5 ST PETERS CHURCH
The church dates mainly from the 13th century, the Lady Chapel being the earliest part. There are some fine 14th century brasses.

7.6 PUBLIC HOUSES
Many, including The Swan and The Kings Arms on the High Street, and The Crystal Palace, The Boat and The Rising Sun on the canal.
Refreshments can also be obtained at the Castle Tea Rooms.

8. BOURNE END
The village is dominated by the A41 and by its industrial area, but has some attractive houses and a church designed by Gilbert Scott. It has two public houses, The Anchor and The White Horse.

9. BOVINGDON

9.1 BRICKWORKS
This brickworks, originally established here in the late 1930s, is the last remaining in Hertfordshire. Local clay is used to make the bricks and 120,000 per week are produced. Some are still made by hand.

9.2 ST LAWRENCES CHURCH
This attractive flint church was built in 1845 on ancient foundations. It contains the effigy of an unknown knight, ca 1370.

9.3 VILLAGE
Bovingdon is an ancient village, once part of the Bailiwick of Hemel Hempstead. The Well House at the crossroads was built in 1881 and its history can be read on the roof beams.

9.4 PUBLIC HOUSES
Several, including The Wheatsheaf, The Royal Oak, The Bell and The Bull.

10. BOXMOOR

10.1 VILLAGE
This is an old village, now surrounded by the town of Hemel Hempstead. It was near Boxmoor that in 1800 a highwayman, Robert Snooks, stole more than £500 in banknotes from the postman. Despite a reward of £300, it was two years before he was caught. He was hanged on 11th March 1802, near to the scene of his crime, and is said to have been the last highwayman hanged in this country.

10.2 MOOR
This is common land, held by the Boxmoor Trust. In season it is grazed by the Trust's small flock of Soay sheep and herd of Belted Galloway cattle.

10.3 PUBLIC HOUSES
Several, including The Fishery Inn and The Steamcoach.

11. BRIDEN'S CAMP
The origin of the name of this tiny hamlet is obscure. It has one public house, The Crown and Sceptre.

12. BUCKLAND

12.1 ALL SAINTS CHURCH
The church was heavily altered in the Victorian period, but is originally 13th century.

12.2 PUBLIC HOUSE
The Rothschild Arms at Buckland Cross

13. RIVER BULBOURNE
The river runs from just north of Dudswell to join the River Gade at Two Waters, a distance of just over 7 miles. It runs alongside the Grand Union Canal and has been used for watercress beds as well as the existing trout farm at Bourne End.

14. CHESS VALLEY

14.1 LATIMER VILLAGE
A delightful village of picturesque cottages around a green. Sir Gilbert Scott, the architect, called it 'a little paradise' when he was here in 1867 to renovate the church (St Mary Magdalene). To the west of the church is Latimer House, rebuilt in 1863. This was the home of Lord Chesham but is now a training college for the Ministry of Defence.

14.2 OLD FLAUNDEN CHURCH
The mediaeval church on this site was abandoned in 1838 when the new church was built in Flaunden village. Only the overgrown foundations remain.

14.3 LIBERTY GRAVE
The tomb of William and Alice Liberty. A bricklayer by trade, William was buried here in 1777, to be joined by his wife in 1809. They both wished to be buried here in the orchard of their old home, near the old church and with a view down the valley they loved.

14.4 RIVER CHESS
The Chess rises above Chesham Vale but remains mostly underground until it emerges at Chesham, then flowing through Rickmansworth to join the River Colne. Its valley is peaceful now, but the river used to provide power for several mills. Originally these were for grinding corn but more recently were converted for paper making. There is a waymarked Chess Valley Walk, with leaflets available from the Countryside Management Service.

15. CHIPPERFIELD

15.1 THE COMMON
The Common has had a chequered history. Originally it formed part of the Royal Manor of Kings Langley, but it passed out of royal ownership in the 16th century. It was sold to the local authority in 1936 'for the purpose of a public open space' and is now managed by Dacorum Borough Council.
Points of interest include two prehistoric round barrows, the very old sweet chestnut trees, and the Apostles Pool, surrounded by twelve lime trees. The smallest of these, 'Judas Iscariot', is a replacement for the original tree which blew down. The pond was used for meditation and fishing by the Dominican Friars from Kings Langley Priory, who also gathered firewood here. Tradition says that Richard III stopped under a chestnut tree to curse the women of the village for mocking his hump. Leaflets for the Chipperfield Common Heritage Trail are available from Dacorum Borough Council.

15.2 ST PAULS CHURCH
The church was built in 1837 by public subscription. It is unusual in that the chancel lies to the west.

15.3 CHIPPERFIELD HOUSE
This is a large private house built in the 19th century.

15.4 MANOR HOUSE
The house to the south-east of the Common, originally called Pinglesgate House, was a lodge of the Royal Palace at Kings Langley. It was probably built in the 16th century but was refronted in Queen Anne style in the 18th century. Rhododendrons in the garden are said to be the first to be planted in England after being brought from China.

15.5 VILLAGE
There are some interesting houses in The Street. Pale Farm, where the Quaker William Penn is said to have stayed, is the oldest house in the village. Both this and the Old Forge are 16th century. The Two Brewers Inn is of similar date and incorporates the former shop, pub and schoolmaster's house. The Church School was built in 1848 and has now been converted into cottages.

15.6 PUBLIC HOUSES
The Two Brewers, The Windmill and The Boot. Nearby at Commonwood is The Cart and Horses.
Refreshments are also available at the tearooms near The Windmill PH.

16. CHOLESBURY

16.1 CAMP
An iron age hillfort on the summit of the Chiltern ridge, Cholesbury Camp extends over about 15 acres. Only earthworks remain, with a triple rampart to the east. Elsewhere the ramparts are double. A triangular outwork at the north west may be the original entrance. Excavations in 1932 revealed seven hearths in the central area, and pottery dating from the early iron age to Romano-British times. At the south west end stands St Lawrence's Church (1873).

16.2 WINDMILL
This was originally built as a smock mill, but its timber structure was found to be unsafe in 1884. It was converted into a tower mill, using the original cap, fantail and machinery but with new sails. It has now been converted into a private residence.

16.3 PUBLIC HOUSE
The Full Moon

17. COW ROAST
There is a well-equipped marina here for canal users, and a Public House nearby on the old A41.

18. DRAYTON BEAUCHAMP

ST MARYS CHURCH
This isolated church, built in dressed stone and flint, is 13th and 14th century, with 15th century stained glass.

19. DUDSWELL

19.1 FORGE COTTAGE
The cottage was built around 1901 and the forge, which was situated in the back garden, was used for shoeing canal barge horses. One blacksmith, Albert Pocock, shod as many as 100 horses per week.

19.2 STABLES
This large brick building was originally used for stabling canal barge horses. The old house near the bridge was once a public house called The Swan, but was closed in 1884 when the landlord was imprisoned for 'misdemeanours'!

20. FLAMSTEAD
This is a charming village with many ancient buildings. There are 16th and 17th century cottages, including 17th century almshouses. The old school, now a private house, is behind the church.

20.1 ST LEONARDS CHURCH
This church was heavily restored in the 19th century but retains features from all periods from Norman to Georgian. There are unusual mediaeval wall paintings and a 15th century screen.

21. FLAUNDEN
Another pretty little village.

21.1 ST MARYS CHURCH
This has the unlikely claim to fame of being the first building designed by Sir Gilbert Scott (in 1838).

21.2 PUBLIC HOUSE
The Green Dragon - note the inn sign!

22. GREAT GADDESDEN

22.1 ST JOHNS CHURCH
The main part of the church is 15th century, though it incorporates Roman bricks which had already been re-used in the earlier Norman building. The tower was rebuilt in 1866, and further restoration work was carried out in the church in 1887. Many members of the Halsey family are buried in tombs in the side chapel.

22.2 RIVER GADE
The river rises at Hudnall Common, then flows for about 20 miles along the Gade Valley. It is joined by the River Bulbourne at Two Waters, then continues to meet the River Chess at Rickmansworth. Due to recent dry summers the river has dried out completely in some stretches.

22.3 GOLDEN PARSONAGE
This house is just a small part of the original building, which dates from 1705. It was the original home of the Halsey family. The name is said to derive from the carpet of daffodils which surrounded the house in Spring.

22.4 VILLAGE
The village goes back to Norman times, when it was known as Gatesdene. A Roman road, now obscured, crosses fields south of the village near Water End, connecting Verulamium with Ivinghoe Beacon (about $13\frac{1}{2}$ miles).

22.5 GADDESDEN PLACE
The house was built in 1770 for the Halsey family by James Wyatt, one of the foremost architects of the 18th century. The inside of the house was destroyed by fire in 1905, but the building survived and was restored three years later. It commands fine views of the Gade Valley, Great Gaddesden and Water End.

22.6 PUBLIC HOUSE
The Cock and Bottle

23. GRAND UNION CANAL

23.1 CANAL
Construction of the canal, formerly known as the Grand Junction Canal, began in 1792 and was completed in 1805 to connect London with the Midlands. In its day it was an important commercial highway, but it is now used mainly for recreation. The many locks in the Chiltern section are needed so that the water level can rise in stages from the Thames valley.
The Wendover Arm is no longer used and it has become dry in some parts, is filled in for agriculture in others and remains wet in the remainder. A Society exists to work towards re-opening the Arm for pleasure activities. The Aylesbury Arm is still in use.

23.2 RESERVOIRS
The four reservoirs are Wilstone, Tringford, Startops End and Marsworth. They were built to supply the Grand Union Canal, but are now also important as a Nature Reserve with a wide variety of resident and migrant birds.

24. GRIMS DITCH

There are several sections of 'Grims Ditch' in Dacorum, not all of which are related. Much of it is probably Iron Age, with some later Saxon sections. The name 'Grims Ditch' derives from the belief that it must have been created by the devil.

25. HEMEL HEMPSTEAD

25.1 NEW TOWN
The New Town is one of seven satellite towns of London planned after the second world war. It was designated a New Town in 1947 and within forty years had quadrupled in population. The main street is Marlowes, with a new shopping centre which was opened in 1990.

25.2 OLD TOWN
There are many interesting buildings in the Old Town, dating from the 17th, 18th and 19th centuries. They include the Old Town Hall, now a thriving Arts Centre, and other buildings focused on the old Market Place. There are several historic public houses. The Old Town is bordered to the west by Gadebridge Park, where excavations revealed a late Roman villa with an exceptionally large bathhouse. Nothing is now visible of this or of a pre-Roman settlement nearby.

25.3 ST MARYS CHURCH
The church is mainly Norman, with late 12th century flint walls. Its spire is nearly 200' high, and it is the largest Norman church in the county, after St Albans Cathedral.

25.4 WATER GARDENS
These gardens along the River Gade were designed by G Jellicoe in 1962-3 to contrast with the busy main thoroughfare.

26. HOCKERIDGE WOOD

This is a mixed deciduous and coniferous plantation on the site of old woodland. The present plantation, designed to combine commercial and recreational use, was started in 1953 and is now managed by the Royal Forestry Society.

27. IVINGHOE BEACON

This is one of the high points of the Chiltern Escarpment and commands magnificent views. The Beacon is surrounded by the ramparts of an Iron Age hillfort, and there are round barrows and other earthworks nearby.

28. JOCKEY END

It appears that the two mile stretch of Gaddesden Row from Jockey End to Stags End may have been used for horse racing. A public house here called The Horse and Jockey was burnt down.

28.1 PUBLIC HOUSES
The Plough, with The Old Chequers Inn further along Gaddesden Row.

29. KINGS LANGLEY

29.1 KINGS LANGLEY LODGE
This building may have been used as a hunting lodge by Charles I : there is a fireplace with the Royal Arms, the initials C.R. and the date 1642.

29.2 PRIORY
The Priory was founded in 1308 by Edward II. A repaired two storey building (not open to the public) is all that remains. Edmund de Langley, son of Edward III, was buried in the Priory Chuch in 1402. The tomb was transferred to the Parish Church in 1574 after the dissolution of the Priory.

29.3 ROYAL PALACE
No remains of the Palace survive above ground, though excavations in 1970 below the Rudolf Steiner School gymnasium revealed part of the old cellar. The Palace was favoured by Edward III as a refuge from the outbreaks of bubonic plague in London, and had an extensive hunting park.

29.4 VILLAGE
A busy village, with various 18th and 19th century buildings.

29.5 ALL SAINTS CHURCH
This is a mainly 15th century church, though with two 13th century alcoves near the altar. As well as the tomb of Edmund de Langley there is a floor brass to the Carter family, ancestors of the former President of the U.S.A.

29.6 PUBLIC HOUSES
Several, including The Royal Palace and The Rose and Crown.

30. LEY HILL COMMON

The common is just part of a much larger wood which once crowned this high ground. There are records of ancient workings here, but no evidence remains today.

31. LITTLE GADDESDEN

31.1 CHURCH OF ST PETER & ST PAUL
This church was built in the 15th century but restored and enlarged in the 19th. It contains many fine monuments to the Dukes of Bridgewater and other owners of the Ashridge Estate. The 3rd Duke is buried here.

31.2 COMMON
There are three memorials on the Common : to Lady Adelaide Brownlow, wife of the 3rd Earl Brownlow; to Lady Marion Alford, who was responsible for the building of the almshouses and other cottages; and the War Memorial. Some beautiful houses overlook the Common, notably the 15th century John o' Gaddesden's House.

31.3 PUBLIC HOUSE
The Bridgewater Arms. This was formerly the village school, but was first licensed in 1815.

32. LITTLE HAY GOLF COMPLEX

This has a position high above the Bulbourne valley, with fine views. It is owned by Dacorum Borough Council and is open for public use, though under private management.

33. LONG MARSTON (WITH GUBBLECOTE)

33.1 VILLAGE
The village pond was the scene in 1751 of the last witch-lynching in England, when Ruth Osborn was drowned. One of her tormentors was gibbetted at Gubblecote, close to the moated site of the deserted mediaeval village which can still be seen.

33.2 CHURCHES
The old mediaeval church was pulled down in 1883. Only the tower remains, set in fields with clearly visible traces of ridge and furrow cultivation. Parts of the church fabric were re-used in the new church.

33.3 PUBLIC HOUSES
The Boot and The Queens Head.

34. MARKYATE

This is a pleasant village along the line of Old Watling Street, originally a Roman Road. Most of the houses are faced with red and grey brick. St John's Church dates from 1734. There are several public houses.

34.1 MARKYATE CELL

The site was originally occupied by a Benedictine Nunnery, founded in 1145 by Abbot Geoffrey of St Albans. Humphrey Bourchier built a manor house here in 1539, parts of which were incorporated in 1825 into the mock Elizabethan mansion now standing.

35. MARSWORTH

35.1 ALL SAINTS CHURCH

The church was started in the 14th century, altered in the 15th and then partly rebuilt in the 19th. Some unusual features are preserved, including brasses and a tomb chest.

35.2 PUBLIC HOUSES

The Angler's Retreat, The White Lion and The Red Lion.

36. NORTHCHURCH

Northchurch was once more important than Berkhamsted, but has now been overtaken. There are some attractive half-timbered houses.

36.1 ST MARYS CHURCH

The church was started in Saxon times and is the oldest in the area, though its tower is 15th century and other parts are later. The grave of Peter the Wild Boy is in the churchyard, with an account of his life on a brass in the church.

37. PICCOTTS END

This is a quiet hamlet that became famous in 1953 when 15th century wall paintings depicting religious scenes were discovered in one of a group of cottages. It appears that the whole row may have been a pilgrims hostel or other important building connected with the monastery at Ashridge.
The cottages were later used by Sir Ashley Paston Cooper, surgeon to King George IV, to establish the first cottage hospital in England in 1826. After about six years the hospital moved to a larger site in Marlowes.

37.1 PUBLIC HOUSES

The Boar's Head and The Marchmont Arms.

38. POTTEN END AND NETTLEDEN

These two parishes have been linked since 1894.

38.1 Potten End has several times won the Hertfordshire Best Kept Village Competition.

38.2 Nettleden used to be on the main road to Ashridge, which crossed the brick bridge over the deeply cut lane leading to Frithsden. Both were built by the Duke of Bridgewater. Many of the cottages here are 17th century, but St Lawrences Church was rebuilt in the 19th century following a fire.

38. **PUBLIC HOUSES**
The Plough and The Red Lion at Potten End, and the Alford Arms at Frithsden.

39. PUTTENHAM

Puttenham takes its name from the de Puttenham family, who occupied the manor for four centuries before the accession of Elizabeth I. It was once a compact village with the church at its centre.

39. **ST MARYS CHURCH**
The earliest parts of the church, including the flint chequer-work, are 14th century. The tower is 15th century.

40. RIDGEWAY PATH

This is a designated Long Distance Path, running for 85 miles from Overton Down in Wiltshire to Ivinghoe Beacon. The route may have been in use for 5,000 years, using high ground to connect the Marlborough and Berkshire Downs with the Chilterns.

41. ROSEHALL WOOD AND MOAT

The site of the former Rosehall Manor is now covered by woodland. The Moat, also overgrown, predates the Manor and may be Roman : it was probably part of the defences of a private dwelling.

93

42. STUDHAM

42.1 THE COMMON
Half of the Common was once in Hertfordshire and was enclosed in 1846. The other half is still common land, and local residents retain rights of furze-cutting and gravel-extraction. During the 19th century nearly all the land came into the Ashridge Estate, but it is now mostly privately owned.

42.2 VILLAGE
The village was wholly transferred to Bedfordshire in 1871. It is still in two parts : Church End, with the church, vicarage, Manor house and a few cottages; and the village, which is mostly small cottages. To the south is the manor and farm of Barworth, formerly Barwythe. Studham declined in prosperity from 1871 due to the disappearance of the straw plaiting industry.

42.3 PUBLIC HOUSES
The Bell and The Red Lion.

43. TRING

43.1 CHURCH OF ST PETER & ST PAUL
The parish church was built largely in the 15th century with extensive restoration in the 19th. It houses memorials to many local notables, especially those connected with Tring Park and Pendley Manor. Others include Sir William Gore, a former Lord Mayor of London, and the Washington family, ancestors of the former President of the U.S.A.

43.2 MANSION
The Manor of Tring is mentioned in the Domesday Survey. It was in Royal hands from then until the reign of Charles I, when it passed to Colonel Guy and the Mansion was rebuilt to a design by Christopher Wren. It passed through several hands before being acquired by the first Lord Rothschild in 1872. The second Lord Rothschild lived there until his death in 1937. The house was then used by the N.M. Rothschild Bank before becoming a private school.

43.3 OBELISK
This monument is reputed to have been erected on the site of the house built by Colonel Guy for Nell Gwynne.

43.4 STUBBINGS WOOD
The bridleways in this wood form part of the Tring Bridleway Circuit, which is sponsored by Dacorum Borough Council.

43.5 TOWN
Tring has a long history as a market town, and still has a Monday cattle market as well as a fruit and vegetable market on Fridays. It has many Victorian buildings and attractive narrow streets.

43.6 ZOOLOGICAL MUSEUM

Tring Museum was built at the end of the last century to house the large and valuable zoological collection of the second Lord Rothschild. The museum opened to the public in 1892, displaying only the finest specimens from all over the world. It was bequeathed to the nation in 1938, and is now part of the British Museum (Natural History).

The Museum is open Monday - Saturday 10 am - 5 pm, Sundays 2 pm - 5 pm. (Admission free at certain times.)

43.7 PUBLIC HOUSES

Several, including the Rose and Crown.
Refreshments are also available at various coffee shops and restaurants.

44. WIGGINTON

44.1 ST BARTHOLOMEWS CHURCH

This is a late Victorian rebuilding of a mediaeval church.

44.2 PUBLIC HOUSE

The Greyhound.

45. WILSTONE

45.1 This small village has few large houses and little now remains of the open green. Wilstone was formerly a chapelry attached to the mother church of Tring, hence Chapel Field and Chapel Farm House at the south of the village.

45.2 PUBLIC HOUSE

The Half Moon.

46. WINKWELL

This is a tiny hamlet set on the canal, with a manually operated swing bridge to allow boats to pass through.

46.1 PUBLIC HOUSES

The Three Horseshoes (16th century), with The Anchor and The White Horse at nearby Bourne End.

NOTES